Vilna, The End of the Road

Sarah Shimonovitz

Producer & International Distributor
eBookPro Publishing
www.ebook-pro.com

Vilna, The End of the Road
Sarah Shimonovitz

Translation from Hebrew: Helene Hart

Edited and translated to Hebrew from the original in Yiddish: Nathan Livneh.

The Hebrew edition was published in 1989 by the author's daughter Zuta-Averbach-Shimonovitz and under the auspices of The association of jews from Vilna and vicinity in Israel.

Contact: Shaul Goffer, sgoffer@bezeqint.net
ISBN 9798788747071

VILNA, THE END *of* THE ROAD

SARAH SHIMONOVITZ

The original manuscript of the book was written by the author in Yiddish and portions were published in newspaper in 1963.

The Hebrew edition of the book was published in 1989. Edited and translated by Nathan Livneh from the Yiddish manuscript.

This book is a translation of the Hebrew edition. The photographs were added to this English edition.

1

June 22, 1941. The Germans performed a surprise attack on the western territories of the USSR, immediately bombing Vilnius, now the capital of Lithuania, among other targets, too. When the frightening, wailing siren was sounded, before the aerial bombing began, I ran out of the house, as I would always do before the war. In those days, when Vilnius belonged to Poland, I was a commander of the Civil Defense against gas and air strikes and told the Polish neighbors in the street, "Perhaps it's a drill." [1]

"*No Pani*,"[2] one of them replied, "the Germans are attacking the Soviet Union, and they've already bombed a number of other cities."

I felt so silly. Instead of providing information, as a former commander should, I was being told something I hadn't imagined. Indeed, the Polish were much more aware of what was about to happen than we Jews were.

---

1 As originally was planned

2 Pani is Polish for Ma'am

The German attack on the Russians wasn't at all sudden, as many believed then and still believe and write to this day. In any case, it was not at all unexpected in Vilnius, my city. Even earlier, we'd heard the underground thunder that later gave rise to a volcanic eruption; just three months earlier, the Germans poisoned the city's drinking water, in an attempt to paralyze the Russian resistance and fighters in Vilnius. As a result, an abdominal typhus epidemic broke out, which resembled a cholera epidemic, and incapacitated many victims.

The hospitals were full of patients; the Russian garrison had been moved far away from the city; only freight trains carrying chlorine from the central Soviet Union were running on railroad tracks to Vilnius - that's what Vilnius looked like for a while before the German attack. One could say that the writing was on the wall. But the Russians didn't understand that. They didn't catch what was happening.

What we, the Jews feared - without even knowing or understanding what was about to happen - had materialized. The Germans had arrived. We already knew that they planned to annihilate the Jews, in any way possible. When I say "we knew," I mean mostly the youngsters, including my son. Anyone who could and dared to, marched off to the Russian border. We, the Jews who stayed here, were no longer thinking about typhus and cholera, or other similar "trifles." The revolution of God had befallen us and the world had darkened for us.

For the Jews of Vilnius, the Germans brought with them the inferno itself, in all kinds of strange and different forms. And they deluged us every day, and in increasing quantities.

All at once, we became completely defenseless people, or more precisely: mice in a trap.

And if the Germans weren't enough, auxiliary forces, gangs of murderers rose up, who thoroughly enjoyed serving as the "weapon bearers" of their German masters in the murdering of Jews. First in line, in the light of day, were the Lithuanian shooters. They called themselves the Ypatingas (Ypatingasis būrys; the special squad). They wanted to be more Nazi than the Nazis, and started catching Jews and shooting them on the street.

Then they began to remove the Jews from their homes. They surrounded entire neighborhoods and quarters, and removed all of the men, supposedly to work, except that they were led to Ponary. "And none who went there had returned." Here, too, they started "small." First, they shot individual Jews. Then dozens and hundreds. They reached thousands. The ground was drenched with blood. Even the sky turned red and hung over our heads. The Jews of Vilnius were already prepared to go into a closed ghetto, provided they could stay alive; survive. After all, in the free world, death lurked on every corner, so it was better to stay alive in the cramped and smelly ghetto, like cockroaches hiding in holes and cracks. That's the entire theory of survival in a nutshell!

One day, the Ypatingas kidnappers burst into our place and took my younger brother, Zelig. He was just 28 years old, full of life and with a head full of plans to be saved and to save. They let him go out first, but while doing so, they punched him in his back and sides. He moved like a drunkard, barely waving a hand at me in parting. In the street, he was sent to join other Jewish youngsters who had been removed from their homes. They were led straight to the Ponary forest, the burial ground of thousands of Vilnius Jews. It was his last journey, together with the others. I didn't know about it at the time. I believed, for some reason, that he was taken to the Lukiški Prison, where the Jews who were caught later were taken. I tried to find a way to get him out of there, but it was not at all an easy task.

I went to the Ypatingas. I also returned to other institutions, but all doors were closed to the Jews. Shut your mouth, Jew. Disappear. No one will listen to you. But I'd decided to save my brother, no matter what. And so, I ran around in despair and stumbled into the office of the German national police on Ostrobramska Street. I walked straight into the lion's den. A few Germans in uniform were sitting around. A man of about 40, who seemed to be in charge, spoke to me. He was a typical German officer, a prototype, like his great-great-great-grandfather. Relaxed, he listened quietly to me, and remarked that my German had a different ring to it than his German, and that I could talk to him, if I wished, in Russian, Polish, or even in the holy language. I preferred that he answer me in Hebrew. And indeed, he spoke in Hebrew and explained to me that in regard to my brother, he was unable to help. It was the Lithuanians' business. He advised me to return home and not to wander about the streets: If my brother survived, he would return on his own. "Just so that you know," he spoke terribly clearly, "what they do with the Jews is the final word on behalf of the Führer." And to make sure that I fully understood him, he assured me that all of the plagues that Pharaoh once received from the Jews in Egypt would be repaid to them with interest by the German government. "But don't worry," he finally ended his lecture to me saying in Hebrew,"Our hope is not lost". I left there in one piece. I went home and wracked my brain: *Who could that German be?*

After only a few days under Nazi rule in Vilnius, days of horror and atrocities, the Lithuanian police burst in on us early in the morning. It was Saturday, September 6, 1941. They ordered us to vacate the apartment. To this purpose, they had allocated us fifteen minutes. We were allowed to take whatever belongings we could carry, and in that, they were doing us a great kindness, which not every Jew was given. After precisely fifteen minutes, our apartment, with everything in it, was shut and locked. It no longer belonged to us. We found ourselves on the street together with many other Jews.

We were led to the ghetto allocated to us.

Thousands of Jews, old and young, walked through the streets of Vilnius with bundles and sacks on their shoulders. We walked crowded together, with the Lithuanian police on both sides. They led us to the Jewish neighborhoods like herds of cattle, urging us to hurry. "Move your butts," they urged us loudly. "The ghetto there is already ready for you." The Jews of all those streets[3] : Szpitalna, Strashun, Lidzki, Jatkowa, Glezer, Zydowska, Niemiecka and Oszmianska had been removed from their homes a few days before, on September 1, and led to Ponary.

3 The names of the streets of the ghetto as they appear in the book are mainly their Polish names or as they were pronounced in Yiddish at that time.

There, they were shot on the edge of and into the pits. In those narrow streets and houses, in which the pure souls of thousands of Jews who'd been murdered were still hovering, they were imprisoning thousands of other Jews. The air there was saturated with Jewish blood. A slaughterhouse, which I had had the opportunity to see at some time in my life, hung before my eyes.

My husband, my daughter and I, laden with a few suitcases and parcels, finally reached the end of the difficult and tedious road. We were now in the ghetto. They drove us into the yard of 9 Lidzki Street. All the yards in the neighborhood were packed full of Jews. Where would we lay our heads? But everyone crowded together, somehow. There was an atmosphere of mourning in the air, that Saturday, the first day in the ghetto.

At midnight, the Lithuanian police closed our street and isolated us from the other streets in the ghetto. Immediately afterward, they started to move us, thousands of Jews, straight to the Lukiški Prison. From there, the path to Ponary was clear.

The way from Lidzki to the prison was terrible. They urged us to "move it," to walk fast. They hit Jews, trying to force them to throw their "unnecessary" suitcases and parcels aside. After all, that is what the eager Lithuanians meant by Jewish property. On the corner of Nowogródzka and Zawalna, a mountain of Jewish parcels and bundles piled up. And on the corner of Pohulanka and Mostova as well. Lithuanian police roamed the streets in trucks and loaded them with loot. It was raining gold for them that day, for those robbers and murderers, they should only choke on the vast Jewish property that fell to them from the heavens.

We were taken from Mostova straight to the prison. To the courtyard. There were already a great number of Jews who'd arrived before us crowding in. And here, too, was the same show: mountains of bundles belonging to Jewish victims who got there before us. An indescribable show of horror. It seemed to me like choked, stifled Jewish sobs could be heard from every bundle.

We were led to a second prison courtyard, and a third, and a fourth, where a large building sprawled. We were ordered inside. It was the prison hospital. It too, was full of Jews who'd been brought there from the ghetto and the city. Many of the Jews of Vilnius were not transported to the ghetto that day, but rather straight to the prison. As it turned out later, every single cell and hole there were full of thousands of Jews. Those who came after them were subsequently "stored" in the prison hospital and many remained in the courtyard. Women and children were sent into the hospital. The men were imprisoned in some other building. During the night, it poured with rain.

The few rooms of the hospital were terribly crowded. Children, big and small, were crying constantly. They were hungry. Their mothers cried with them. We were all overwhelmed with desperation. It was a waking nightmare. It proclaimed the coming of the next day, a day as dark as that night in the prison. There may have been a few "happy" people among the Jews there, who wouldn't make it to the next day...

The next day, representatives of German factories arrived to take their Jewish laborers from the prison. But not many Jews worked in German factories. Most of those were simple people; all-year-round Jews who would never return to Lukiški or to the ghetto. They would be led to Ponary to be shot there.

It was the second day of the week. We'd been in prison for two days. My daughter and I and a few other women left the hospital, which was full of the sobs and moans of desperate women and children. We joined our husbands in another courtyard. They started by registering professional people who had proof on them of their profession. They and their families would be returned to the ghetto. Immediately, groups were formed of people who stood a chance of being saved. Physicians, engineers, technicians, metal workers, carpenters, and others. My husband was not among those groups. He didn't work for some German unit. We belonged to the thousands of Jews who were being shot in Ponary in those days.

And then we were given a chance, or perhaps it was a miracle. Our daughter was registered in a group of professionals. She was not, however, allowed to take us, her parents, with her. We had no choice. We had to say goodbye. She refused, while I begged her to go: She had to be saved, if possible. What would it have helped if she'd stayed with us? On the other hand, the fact that she was to remain alive would have made it easier for us to die. Crying, she said goodbye to us. Those on the list were removed from the courtyard, sent closer to the exit gate. Thousands of pairs of eyes followed them as they walked. With tears in her eyes, my daughter pleaded with the Lithuanians from the prison administration, who were passing by, to spare her parents and allow them to go with her. The Lithuanians laughed at her, mimicking the way she cried. After all, it was such a golden opportunity to get rid of the Jews, and that girl just stood there driving them up the wall regarding her old parents. The group was now standing by the exit gate. They checked the papers they were holding again.

My daughter kept begging all of the prison officials. Some answered her mockingly. She stood with the group, and to us, it felt like she was watching as we were being shot into the pit. She closed her eyes so as not to see. Suddenly, one of the officials come over to her and asked her what her parents' names were and where they were, and he came immediately to get us out. When a person wants to save and free someone, he's not lazy. He went to look for me and my husband and added our names to the list. She had found a single righteous person in Sodom, or perhaps one of the 36 hidden righteous people… But it is hard to believe that so many righteous individuals still existed then…

They opened the gate for us and we were led out, together with all the professionals, back to the first ghetto. Could anyone in the world be as happy as we were?

2

At first, the ghetto was divided in two. There was probably a reason, and it made it easier for them to control us.

The stuffiness and crowding in the apartments, the dirt and grime, the murderous attacks by the Lithuanian police - was all unbearable. To this day, it's hard for me to understand how we could live like that.

My husband worked at a Lithuanian institution and was given an *Artbeitsschein* - a work permit.

It stated that he and his family were permitted to live in Ghetto A, which included the streets Rudnicka, Szpitalna, Strashun and Jatkowa, and the alleys like Szawelska, Oszmianska and Dysnos. Ghetto B included the streets and alleys on the other side of Niemiecka street like: Zydowska, Jatkowa and Glezer.

Very soon, people started moving between the two ghettos. People without *Schein* - who also did not belong to families with *Scheins*, were forced to move to another ghetto. That was the ghetto's Jewish police officers' job. To this day, I can't forget the horrifying image of how the ghetto police removed an elderly lady holding a small bundle from her home. She could barely walk and was helpless. She knew she was being led to her death. A girl of about eight ran after her, crying and shouting, "Grandma, Grandma, why are they taking you away from us?"

Not much time passed before Ghetto B was wiped out. A few thousand Jews from there had already been executed in Ponary. Now the Germans were beginning to look into what was happening in Ghetto A. It seemed to them that there were too many Jews in the ghetto. As such, they issued new *Scheins* to a limited number of people. All the rest, the redundant, were to be executed, and the sooner the better. For that purpose, huge pits had already been dug in Ponary. In order to prevent mistakes, the new *Scheins* were printed on yellow paper, to differentiate them from the old ones, which were printed on white paper. My husband had not yet received a new *Schein*. He was an accountant by profession, and the Germans didn't need accountants.

All the "redundant" people learned immediately that that's what they were. The angel of death's scythe was already shimmering before their eyes. And indeed, on the night of October 24, the Gestapo decree was issued, stating that all the Jews with yellow *Scheins* were to leave for work early in the morning, together with their families: the husband, his wife, and up to four children. And that's what happened. The happy yellow *Schein* holders left the ghetto with their families. Other yellow *Schein* holders closed themselves up in some Judenrat building on Rudnicka Street. All the other miserable people, many thousands of Jews, remained in the ghetto - prey for the Lithuanian beasts, who would rip them apart with their rifles and pistols and drown them in their own blood.

The large courtyard at 1 Szawelska Alley was allocated for those redundant people, those with white *Scheins*. But the white *Schein* holders knew that they were being cornered. That it was a trap. And they avoided going there. Instead, they hid in the ghetto wherever they could, sticking with supposed relatives or friends who were among the happy ones. But their good friends weren't thrilled to be connected to the "Whites" and they were reluctant to do so. The distinguished yellow *Schein* holders were of the opinion that the "white Jews" were destined for extermination, that they were just getting under their feet and had no chance of surviving; they were merely risking the innocent lucky yellow *Schein* holders.

Two women with yellow *Scheins* were standing in the courtyard by the faucet. They were filling their containers with water and talking between themselves. One of them complained about the lice and bedbugs in the ghetto. The other replied, "My dear, the Whites are worse than the lice."

I felt a vibration in my guts: Is that really a Jewish woman? Are they all like that? Is the human being really better than the beasts? And if so, - what direction are we going in?

But even the unfortunate want to live. A few people somehow managed to escape the ghetto in this and that way while putting themselves in danger. Some of them tried to reach the Russian border, believing it was safer there. Others hid in attics, basements and camouflaged holes. In the ghetto, they were called *malinas*, or hiding places.

My son was forced to come back; It was two days before the yellows and the whites were separated. The German army got there before he and the other youngsters escaped into the Soviet Union. And because of that, he decided to go to the forests and he came to say goodbye to us. My daughter went with him. She wanted to help him through the dangerous places.

And what about us?

My son and daughter were outside the ghetto, and my husband and I looked for a place to hide. We didn't have a *malina* in our own, so we went to friends who were in the same boat. They were hiding in the deep basement of a house at 6 Strashun Street. There, we met other people that we knew.

About 50 Jews were hiding in those well-disguised basements. I read a fictitious story once, about people living in houses deep at sea. We were literally living deep in the Earth, without daylight. "From the depths, I cried unto the Lord" became the most popular prayer in the *malinas*, but there was no lack of dark humor, either.

It was a warm and sunny day. The streets of the ghetto were empty.

I looked at the people in the *malina* and listened to what they had to say. They weren't a desperate mob or a toy in the hands of fate. They were people coming along in years, in the prime of their lives, and youngsters, energetic and bold, willing to fight for their lives. The Gestapo, lords of the sun and of the air, demanded the heads and blood of the Jews who were sitting in darkness and in the shadow of death; the heads of the Judenrat, who actually believed that if they handed over thousands of healthy, lively and energetic young Jews to the murderers, they would be allowed to live.

Two female students were sitting in the corner. Someone was going to bring them Aryan documents but was too late. Others were discussing how to escape to White Russia. There, they believed, the situation was much better than in the Vilnius ghetto. The main thing was to get through that fateful day in peace.

My husband sat in the *malina* and did calculations of his own as to how we could survive; how we could avoid despair and hysteria. In his humble opinion, it would have helped if we had a flask of hot tea with us. Who knew how long we'd have to sit there? As it was so quiet in the ghetto, "not even a leaf was moving," I left the *malina* and went up to Szawelska Street, which is where we lived, to fill the flask with tea. A lot of people were hiding there, too, in the courtyards. The quiet before the storm seemed to be hanging in the air. It was frightening. I filled the flask and then heard a shout from a lookout point: "The Lithuanians! The dogs are coming!" I rushed out to the street. A gang of Lithuanians were already at work on the other side of Strashun Street. They spread out into yards 2, 3, 4, 5 and 6, and I had no way of getting back to "my" *malina*. I stopped for a moment, bewildered and at a loss. But I quickly regained my senses and went into the stairwell of 15 Strashun Street. The sudden fear drove me all the way up the stairs, to the roof. There, I crawled up to a platform hidden by a number of planks and a basket. That's where I sat down to rest. It was midday. The sun was warm and shining on the roofs around me. It was a strangely pastoral picture. For a moment, I imagined myself sketching it...but then the fear returned to attack me. Those dogs, with their sense of smell! And indeed, down there in the narrow alleys, the horrific and bloody attacks against the hiding, defenseless Jews had begun.

The Lithuanian police officers broke the locked gates, broke the doors and the windows. I could hear the sound of shattering glass panes, the sound of the crying and shouting voices of people being removed from their hiding places. They were chased and dragged out of the *malinas*, jabbed and battered by fists and rifle butts. Those poor, misfortunate people, whose bitter luck was to be born Jewish. I could also hear shooting. They were probably shooting anyone who was having difficulty walking or was refusing to run. I sat on the platform, which seemed to have been raised just in time for me. The Lithuanians were walking through the apartments beneath me. rummaging around in their search, they opened cabinets, broke dishes, serving ware and windowpanes. Eventually, they left. From where I was sitting, I could see people - sorry, Jews - crawling on the boiling hot, sloping roofs, like born acrobats. The fight to live was extremely frightening. Below, in the narrow alleys, the horrific pogrom was still going on. From where I was, I couldn't see it, but I could hear the crying and screams of terror of people being beaten. The sun was warming me with great amicability, as if to cause anger. It didn't care what was being done in the dark and narrow alleys below. My children were always drawing the sun laughing, grinning from ear to ear. Now I could see it clearly like that. I wanted to explode. In my mind, I began to summarize God's reports on humanity, on the world; on our situation in the ghetto. I hoped it would calm me down a little, but it didn't. I quickly found myself at odds with all the do-gooders in the world, with their lofty statements but who didn't lift a finger to prevent clean and pure blood from spilling. Quite the contrary. They held their peace as if giving their permission…where were they, those people preaching justice and mercy all of the time, the brotherhood of nations? Who was the sun shining for here in the ghetto?!

The horrific day was coming to an end. Heavy clouds covered the sky and it started to rain. In the ghetto, the pogrom subsided. The last victims, those that the Lithuanians, the dogs sniffed out and found later, left in tears.

There was the sound of a sharp whistle to signal the dogs, and they left the ghetto. They'd had their fill for the day. The remaining Yids had nowhere left to run. They could continue the following day.

I came down from my hiding place and ran to the *malina* at 6 Strashun Street. The *malina* had been broken into and there was no sign of life, no trace of the people who had been there. All the basements were pitch dark. I shouted out and my voice echoed through the empty basements. Slowly more and more, happier people emerged from the *malinas* that had "survived." They groaned at the great catastrophe that had befallen so many Jews, and dispersed each person to their own "home." There was no sign of my husband, of my friends, of my acquaintances. I was left all on my own. I remember a saying in Hebrew, *Gadol shivri ke'yam* - I am as shattered as the sea is big. This time, it was no mere flowery phrase.

The next day, my daughter came to the ghetto. We tried to find a way to save Dad and our friends. My daughter ran to the Lithuanians for whom my husband worked. She begged them to save Dad, who was in prison, but they got there a little too late. Dad was no longer there...

3

The terror and nightmares followed one another. Once again, my son had not returned to the ghetto.

Before November 1, he sent a note to me. He was leaving on foot for Lida. He wrote further that he didn't know where he would find his end. But as long as he was alive, he wouldn't be led to Ponary.

Night fell. The next day was the Christian holiday, All Saints Day of 1941. It started snowing and then snowing harder. I stood at the window. My son was on his way, walking on foot. And what a way it was! I walked with him, with all my senses and with every part of my body. I didn't feel the cold by the window. The way was full of dangers. They lurked there, waiting for him every step of the way. I protected and guarded him, so that he would arrive safely at his destination. The snow kept on falling.

Once again, rumors spread of a new "selection" in the ghetto, for people who had white *Scheins*, which had long not been valid. The previous attack, on October 24, in which thousands of Jews had fallen, was not enough for them. Our murderers were thirsty for more Jewish blood. The pits of Ponary were not yet full enough.

My daughter and I didn't have yellow *Scheins*. Again, I wasn't concerned for myself, but rather for how I could save my daughter. For 3,000 rubles, my 16-year-old daughter joined a family with a yellow *Schein*. To that end, I sold my expensive fur. My daughter cried bitterly, refusing to leave me on my own. I explained to her that we would both be caught if we stayed together, whereas if we were each on our own, we may be able to survive, somehow, since we would be freer. My daughter insisted. The "parents" separated us using true force, and she was dragged sobbing behind them.

On November 3, a new edict was issued: All holders of yellow *Scheins* were to move temporarily with their families to the other ghetto, which at the time had already been emptied of Jews.

Where we were, in Ghetto A, a bloody pogrom was about to begin, against the Jews without valid *Scheins*, and all roads from it were closed and sealed for them. My daughter left the ghetto with her *Schein*-holding parents. I remained behind on my own and tried to hide in a *malina,* a storage space in the attic of 10 Rudnicka Street. There were many more people there with me, both old and young and with unfamiliar faces. They fought for every corner and every meager bundle of straw to lay their heads on. People talked constantly. I, for some reason, was particularly sad. The air was stifling. I ask people to let me out and they very willingly agreed. One person less meant more air to breathe.

I walk through the narrow alleyways, where everything was quiet. Few went through the gate. I walked to the

Szawelska alley thinking I may find a place to hide there. Suddenly, I noticed a man and a boy, holding a *Schein*. They were walking toward the gate leading to Jatkowa Street. I asked the man to take me with them, as his wife. He refused, saying that he couldn't. There was no wife recorded on his *Schein*. We talked all the way to the gate. There was one Lithuanian guard there. It was late, and the Lithuanian was tired. Hundreds of Jews had already been sent that day to Ponary by him. He didn't want to read another yellow *Schein*. He was yellow up to his eyes. He just asked: Husband, wife and child? To which I answered, "Yes," and before we knew it, we were passing through the gate and standing in Ghetto B territory.

I wandered through the narrow lanes of Ghetto B. Everything there seemed to be alive with people who only a day or two ago had been led by those police officers "with murder in their eyes" to their brutal death.

The Jews of Ghetto A who had just entered Ghetto B, those "distinguished" yellow *Schein* holders, were staying in empty apartments. People packed bundles of clothes for themselves from those left behind by the Jews who had "gone." Others undressed and put on better clothes. I watched that hideous "carnival" and felt a stinging indignity. I walked around feeling strange and lonely. By chance, I had landed up with the "distinguished." That was twice as hard for me: All the abhorrence and nagging worries. It pierced my mind like a drill: Where had I come to? I spent two difficult days and nights without sleep.

I went with all the yellow *Schein* holders. The examination at the gate, without the Gestapo, was not very strict. I passed through the gate with a group of Jewish railway workers.

In those two days, during which the Germans and the Lithuanian Ypatingas dogs plundered Ghetto A, they executed thousands of Jews who didn't have yellow *Scheins* and led them to be shot into the pits. Elderly and middle-aged Jews, youngsters and children. They were truly horrific days, with criminals and murderers acting like gods and sentencing thousands of defenseless Jews.

I found my daughter! When the resurrection comes and parents meet their resurrected sons and daughters, their joy will surely be similar to ours. Oh, how many tears those happy unfortunate people will cry! And we were just like them...

My daughter started to help the person responsible for our yard. His hands tremored with hunger and cold. She did his work for him and in return, she received a permit that she was working, and in those days, the permit was tantamount to a permit to stay alive (for the time being!).

She was permitted; and that temporary permission was given to her not only by our arch enemies, but also by our brethren, whose right to live at all would surely be taken away from them the following day...

From that I learned that the trait of most people, irrespective of religion or race, was to get rid of anyone and anything in their way who might put their lives at danger, even if they weren't a hundred percent sure of it. In this, the human being's cruelty is greater than that of the forest beasts, who are not cruel to their own kind, even in dangerous situations. I have often reflected in my heart: If only I was with animals in the desert, and not people in the ghetto...

It's the eve of the new year, 1942. My daughter and I received a room to live in. At 12 Strashun Street. There was a large courtyard with a lot of people. The other room in the apartment, which was slightly bigger, was given to Reizel Korczak (Rozka), together with other members of the family. And the family - friends from the youth movement Ha-shomer Ha-tsa'ir - was not at all small. Among them were Vitka Kempner, Chaika Grossman, Eliyahu (Edek) Boraks and other refugees fleeing from the Germans in Poland and the Germans got hold of them in Vilnius.

Just before the new year, one of the leaders of Ha-shomer Ha-tsa'ir, Abba Kovner, arrived at the ghetto[4]. We'd known Abba Kovner for years. He was a classmateof my son's, from the Hebrew Gymnasium.

---

4 In January 1942, the United Partisan Organization (Fareynikte Partizaner Organizatsye, FPO) was established in Vilna ghetto,
of which Abba Kovner was one of the leaders and became its commander in July 1943.

4

By the last three months of 1941, the Germans had already murdered all of my closest relatives: my parents, my brother, my husband, my two married sisters - one with her husband and four adult children, and the second, with her husband and two adult children. All in all, fourteen of the people closest to me, besides other family members.

The first German bombing of Vilnius was when my son Michael turned 22. He had graduated from the technical-government high school in Vilnius. Early that morning, he went to take part in a boat and paddle board competition on the Vilia River. He was an excellent swimmer and sailor, and he was truly captivated by sailing.

In the hours before noon, a rain of bombs began to fall from the blue sky all over the city. A bomb fell at the rowing station, too. The sailing competition was stopped in the middle.

The next day, the war was already well underway. My son, along with many other young people like him, walked somewhere, far away. His place was now in the ranks of the resistance against the brutal enemy, the Germans. He walked in the lead taking difficult routes, but at a certain point, they couldn't continue. The Germans, with their automobiles, were faster. After a lot of difficulties and shortcuts along the way, he managed to get back to Vilnius. His face and spirit had dropped. He could see what was coming and it frightened him. He saw himself as a gladiator obligated to fight a ravenous pack of lions. The Germans reached every road and path before him. They blocked every crossing in his way. They popped up on every side like demons from underground. We tried to comfort and encourage one another; the irony of fate.

In the city, he witnessed fear and mourning for the Jewish victims. He, the driven young man and faithful friend, looked for new ways. He made plans. And again: He would not work for the Germans. Sooner or later, they would turn all the people working for them into skin and bones. One couldn't trust the devil. No, his path would lead somewhere entirely different.

We, the Jews of Vilnius, were now imprisoned in the ghetto, with a sword hanging over our heads. It was a gory nightmare. The frequent riots and murders in the ghetto, which as usual they called "*aktions*" in those dark times, sometimes left a big empty space in the younger ranks of the ghetto. With just a stick in hand, there was no way to fight off the predatory lions and wolves.

My son did not let up. He was an inspiration. He called on his friends and acquaintances to go out into the forests, with or without weapons, and to join the soldiers of the Red Army. Weapons, they would find, the main thing was not to sit back and wait for death.

However, his passionate words and appeals with indisputable explanations, was a voice crying in the wilderness. People accepted things then as a utopia, like delusions after despair that make the situation even more dangerous and that lead to self-destruction.

The idea of organizing partisan units in Vilnius to fight the enemy was now beginning to grow, but it had not yet ripened. As such, my son prepared to leave. He used a chemical to delete the word "Jew" in his identity documents, already Russian, and wrote "Tatar" instead. He was fundamentally a Tatar already, except for the blond hair on his head. His name and his father's name could remain as they were: They, too had a Tatar sound to them. He attached his school diploma to his identity documents, as it didn't include any details regarding nationality.

He left Vilnius on November 1, 1941, and headed for the city of Lida in White Russia (Belarus). They had set up a ghetto there, too. For some reason, many of the Jews of Vilnius had fled there, and he went there himself. The way there was very difficult, full of danger and ambushes by murderers of Jews. The aim was to organize a group of partisans in Lida. There was a rumor among the Jewish youth in Vilnius that things were less tedious in Lida. The youth were more aware of what was happening. He also tried to connect with young Christians outside of the ghetto, but failed. He was arrested. "Today, a Tatar bandit was arrested," they informed the public. He understood that the game was lost. And then, he acted like someone with toothache. The awful pain deprived him of the power of speech, and he was unable to answer their questions. A police officer took him to a dental clinic. He escaped and hid in the ghetto in Lida, no longer a Tatar, once again a Jew.

In the spring of 1942, he left with a few friends from Lida. With very few weapons, they went into the forests of White Russia. And neither he or his friends were seen again.

Throughout all the years of the war, the path of the partisans was no bed of roses. The path was even more difficult for the first ones, who paved the way for those who followed. Their path was a bed of spikes and thorns, of pit holes and bumps, of snakes and death. But they fell in a heroic war, like the heroes of Israel in ancient times.

5

September 1943. Again, the Jews of the ghetto were not taken to work outside the ghetto. Because that way, the gate could be closed and no one could come or go. We realized that the liquidation of the ghetto was imminent, and it was possibly the very end.

The Jews of Vilnius tried to guess which death they would choose for us. Some joked in the way they learned a page of the Gemara: If you say that they'll set the ghetto on fire from outside, then the fire could spread to the houses beyond the ghetto, and heaven forbid, endanger the homes of the Christian neighbors, too, and then they would lose more than they would gain, no? But what if they dropped bombs from above? Who would guarantee that the pilot wouldn't miss and drop even a single bomb on their supporters? Say that, quoting the external Mishna, they disperse gunpowder, which they call dynamite, in all kinds of places, and the whole of the Vilnius ghetto blows up to the sky at once, that Vilnius, Jerusalem of Lithuania. As the sages said, the celestial Jerusalem (of Lithuania). Here another Jew, short, skinny and lame, interrupted:

That's true, that's true! And here is the proof: Didn't the Germans blow up with dynamite two high-rise buildings, with their Jews inside, on12, 14 and 15 Strashun Street?

The man making his case defied him: "Look, look, Jews want to joke a little about their troubles, and here he comes and kills them."

The hunger could be seen in everyone's eyes. Like mice in a trap, the Jews started to run around the ghetto, looking for a way to escape. But everything was locked and bolted, and the security was as never before. The Jews started to climb on the walls, to crawl through attics and rooves, basements and sewers. They dug tunnels, crawling underground like moles. And if someone actually managed to find themselves on the other side, they received proof that they had no one to turn to, that they were most unwanted guests, and that they were being looked at with suspicious looks that said: "The police must be notified quickly. We don't want them to stay alive."

Back in the ghetto, I met a woman coming down from the storage space in the ceiling. It was on the same day of the extermination.

"Pani," I asked her, "why are you going down to the ghetto precisely when death is howling at our doors?"

"Oh," she said, and burst into tears, "the Christian world around us wants us gone, they do not have God in their hearts. It's best to die together with my children, with other Jews."

On September 14, the Gestapo called in Jacob Gens, the head of the Vilnius ghetto government, a former Lithuanian army officer under President Smetona. After a short talk with him, the mass murderer of the Vilnius ghetto, Martin Weiss, ordered him, "Proud Jew, turn around!" and Gens replied, "I indeed remain a proud Jew, shoot!" The Gestapo commander shot him and Gens crumbled down in the Gestapo yard. Weiss himself told this to the Jewish workers who were working in his garden.

Now everyone knew: The end was very near. Worry gnawed at us, giving us sleepless nights.

September 23, 1943. It was five days before the Jewish New Year. Dawn had not yet broken and the ghetto was in turmoil and confusion. People were running around like they had lost their minds. They didn't know who, what or when. For a few days, the ghetto had been surrounded by the army, police and all sorts of dogs. The Germans were not lacking in support.

In the morning, everyone knew it was their last day in the Vilnius ghetto. An edict had already been issued for all the Jews to leave the ghetto immediately. They were moving to labor camps in Estonia. Anyone who refused would be shot on the spot. No one mourned for the ghetto, but nor did they believe the German animals. But did they have any other choice? Here - there was death. There - it would come a little later.

The Jews hid in *malinas* that had been prepared in advance for that purpose. But the vast majority threw their bundles over their shoulders and started walking toward the gate.

By then, many Jews from Vilnius who had been removed from the ghetto earlier were already in Estonia.

I was left alone in my small room. There had been people with me - and now they were gone. None of them stayed. Some went to the gate, others to hide. Just a few escaped the ghetto. Only I remained, on my own. What would I do? I'd been in the ghetto for two years. Most of my family, relatives and friends had been murdered during the first months during the selections in the Vilnius ghetto. My son had left the ghetto a long time before and I didn't know where he was or if he was even still alive. I had just said goodbye to my daughter. Her path led through the forest. Her place is with the partisans. Bands of Jewish partisans from Vilnius had long been roaming about the forests. My daughter was among the latest to join. There was no way out. The guards were everywhere. People went out through the sewage system. But then I was informed: My daughter had been caught and sent with other young women and girls to a labor camp in Riga.

I still wondered what to do, whether to go to the gate, as ordered, or to hide in an attic or basement. I did not like the darkness of the *malinas* in the basements. It scared me. I preferred to die in the forests, in a field, with one last look at the sky. To me, it seemed that even lying in a mass grave along with others of your own people was a little happier...and that's what that mother of children meant.

The dice fell on the gate. I packed only the most necessary of items, along with a hand basket and small container of water. I was ready for the trip.

I went down to the courtyard. There were very few people there. An elderly Jewish man was sitting by the window, reciting Psalms. That was all he could do before his death. He had nothing to go on for. He would die here, in the Jerusalem of Lithuania. To him, it was holy land. Generations of the righteous and great rabbis were buried here. His burial site would be with them. A young woman with a baby in her arms was running around, wringing her hands in despair, asking what she should do, where she should go. What could I advise her, in the state she was in? I just told her that I thought it best to go than to run around in the street and wait for the bullet. But she stayed. Maybe she had a place to hide.

I continued on my way, saying goodbye with a glance, without longing or resentment, from the buildings in the ghetto, from the narrow alleyways, from everything around; from the place I had experienced so many problems and endless anguish.

There were still Jews about rushing to the gate with bundles. The executioners could already be seen in the ghetto, on Rudnicka Street. They seemed to be Ukrainians. A new race of executioners. Until now, the two-legged dogs we'd known had been German, Lithuanian, Estonian and Latvian.

They were already searching the courtyards. They rushed the Jews walking to the gate, which now wide open, opposite the Church of All Saints. The Lithuanian police were on both sides. As always, we walked in the middle of the road. The sidewalks were full of Christians. Were they curious to know where the Jews were being taken? They ran us through Subocz Street to Rasu Street. A network of railway tracks led out from there. We were taken to the courtyard of an ancient monastery, the Gestapo Kingdom. The men were run straight into the next courtyard. The women, the elderly and the children were chased into the garden. It started to rain. It was damp and muddy and there were a lot of people from the ghetto in the garden. I could barely find a place to sit. Then evening fell and it grew cold. People curled up into balls, snuggled up; a remedy against the cold. We sat there and dozed off with nagging thoughts. What would tomorrow bring? People were exhausted and weary, and hungry, and wet, and were still trying to delude themselves into believing that they'd perhaps be shown mercy.

Torches had been lit in a few of the corners. They burned all night. Every now and then, a rocket exploded. Whoever was napping woke up shocked with sudden fear. We may have been photographed.

As we knew, Kittel, that Gestapo dog and the executioner of the Vilnius ghetto, was an actor; or an opera singer. And he believed in emotional pictures. He could play freely and undisturbed with the heads and lives of the Jews. He learned to direct people in various states of fear.

September 24. More women were brought to the garden the next day, early in the morning. Perhaps they had despaired from hiding in the *malinas*. Later, the Judenrat families and the Jewish police officers' families were brought in. None of them, heaven forbid, were deprived of privileges. Only a few certain "people of importance" from among them, the "privileged," were sent to the ghetto in Kaunas, which still existed at the time.

The day began. An order was given to move from the garden to another courtyard, or to one of the lanes. We walked slowly. It was very crowded. Horrifying information from the people close to the gate reached us all by word of mouth: The Gestapo had brought in three partisans whom they'd caught, from those who had escaped through the sewers the day before. The three were well known to the public: the lawyer, Abraham Havoinik, , the teacher Jacob Kaplan, and a young female student, Asia Big. They led them to the men's "quarter" in the other courtyard, where the gallows had already been prepared for them. Our three saints parted from the people around them by blowing kisses in the air.

We continued walking from one gate to the next, "protected" by the police. There was much confusion on the other side of the gate, where young women and girls were being separated from the rest of us. Those who went to the right - who knew where they were headed, perhaps to work. And then, there were those who went to the left, probably to the melting furnace. The honorable bloodthirsty Kittel himself was conducting the game. He probably felt that he was in the right role: singer-actor-director. Playing Cain himself. But Cain was nothing compared to him.

The children of the young women were taken to the left. The mothers of young girls were also directed to the left. I, too, was sentenced, to go left. Kittel selected about 1,700 women to go to the right. They were enough for him. He didn't need more. After that, everyone went left: young and old women, children with or without their mothers, the elderly and the sick. We were all heading for the furnace; to become ash. Hell was all around us; people crying and screaming out loud. Their voices seemed to tear the sky apart, reaching the heavens. But the sky was too high. The sun, which suddenly appeared, was so very far from us, and the chill of death had us all in its clutches.

The horrific day was moving ahead, coming to its end. It was already dusk. The group that went right was being led ahead. They knew it would be their one last look, their chance to send regards for the last time. They would be no longer.

I looked around me. Where were we? On one side, there were the high walls of the ancient monastery. The Germans had taken it over a long time ago. They led the monks out and shot them. On the other side, there was a brick fence, well-guarded by the Ukrainian and Lithuanian police. The overcrowding was terrible. But who says that those deemed to die were worthy of being more comfortable? Many of them were crying softly. Others were complaining to God above; to humanity: *What does He up in heaven and those down below want from the miserable Jewish people?*

It grew dark. People were dropping on their bundles, weary and exhausted. They dozed off lying down, or sitting, in whatever which way. I leaned on my bundle, thinking of spending the night like that. What a nightmare it was! Later, after the darkness had thickened, the police officers guarding us, surely from every danger and predicament, started to crawl between the curled up and crowded people sleeping. They took bundles, belongings. They promise to release people for money, or for items of value. They took the victims far away, taking anything that they could from them, and then - there would be a shot. A shout in the dark - and quiet. That was one released. A minute later, they were back, leading the next victim away.

I buried my head deeper in my bundle, like an ostrich, so I wouldn't see or hear, barely breathing. But I could hear every sound, every step, every touch of the killers. There they were, coming closer to me. I thought that they were reaching out their thieving hands toward me. But no. Apparently, I was too poor for them. They moved away. Oh, that dark and dismal night in Rasu, near the old monastery!

Dawn was rising. I rubbed my numb arms and legs. Two women beside me organized their belongings. I guessed they were preparing to escape along the way. I wished them good luck.

We'd already removed our yellow badges. Once again, we had nothing to fear from Kittel, the mass murderer. They wouldn't shoot us a hundred times. It was a waste of bullets.

I too, had not yet completely given up. I had not yet said my last word. I believe that I sang out loud: "Never say this is the final road for you…" The Jewish partisan song...

6

September 25, Saturday morning. We were driven down the street leading to the train. Bundles were tossed about, belongings scattered. Lonely, abandoned children, little orphans, rummaged through them. They must have been hungry and looking for something to eat. We were assigned to groups of 25 and led to the train. I looked around: *Should I perhaps try to escape?* Suddenly, I was hit on the head with a rifle. My eyes grew dark and the new wound started to bleed. I pressed on the wound with a handkerchief and kept going. Before I had time to recover, we were by the train cars. From there, I couldn't escape. The Lithuanian police had done their job. Now the Ukrainians were replacing them. Again, we were counted, 25 times 3, including the ill, all in all 75 heads, and then we were pushed into cattle cars. We were highly overcrowded. One could literally suffocate.

In the car I was shoved into, there were two small hatches at the top. I pushed in among the first and immediately grabbed a spot by the hatch. I stood on my bundle to reach the window and carefully looked out. The Ukrainians, the soldiers of Vlasov, were already guarding the full cars. They were in high spirits. For them, it was a gay funfair. They told us, kindly, that we were being transported to Warsaw, to do easy labor. We would spend four days on the road and they would give us provisions for the journey, bread and water. Decent people…it was a shame that they didn't change positions with us. They added: "Not long ago, we transported throngs of Jews from Estonia, to do the same job in Warsaw.

Indeed, we felt that we could believe them, since perhaps Estonia didn't have death camps like the blessed Godfearing country, Poland.

I continued to peek through the window. The cars were standing in a half circle, and they were attaching more cars; more Jews from the ghetto…men, women, the elderly and young children. They were afraid, frightened to death: Where were they being taken? Where would they be executed? Close by, or a little further away? Either way, they knew that it was their last journey.

I counted the carriages. They were full and crammed to capacity. And still, they couldn't contain all the Jews from the ghetto. Meanwhile, some of them were locked up in a walled building by the train. They would be "given a ride" the next day. I could see them being led there from a distance. It was the same image as the day before: the young, the old, and the children. Some with bundles on their shoulders, some without. Like true sheep to slaughter. I stood there wondering if anyone who hadn't seen it with their own eyes could ever understand it.

Two labor camps with Jews remained in the city: Kailis and the HKP forced labor camps. They had their own gory story later.

Meanwhile, the locomotive was brought closer. It turned out that my car was the closest to the locomotive. Only the Ukrainian guards' open car was between us. They were most unsympathetic neighbors. Our sages, may they rest in peace, were right when they said, "Distance yourselves from a bad neighbor." And indeed, our sages also advised to run away from them. The idea to run away didn't leave me. I couldn't escape through the door. That left the hatch. I was thin enough, mere skin and bone. And if I wasn't shot beforehand, I was going to try my luck in the dark of night. Maybe God will have mercy on me…

In the meantime, the Vlasovscis were doing business. Here, one of them was selling the train operator a gold watch for a bottle of vodka. He must have just stolen the watch from a Jew. Others were carrying bundles around and looking for railroad workers to negotiate with.

Two Christian girls were asking the Ukrainians something. And then they were in my car. They took the shoes off two of the women: "You don't need them anymore," and gave them to the young Christian girls, who were waiting by the car.

It was deafeningly noisy in the car and no one could hear each other. The happy ones, who had their bundles, sat on them. Others stood crammed together. I scanned my partners in fate, some familiar, some not. Privileged women from the ghetto were sitting in the opposite corner: the mother of Jacob Gens with her relatives, women from Vilnius and from Lithuania. They were saying something, but no one could hear what or what about.

Outside, they warned us to sit quietly, not to peek through the "windows." Otherwise, they would shoot and close the shutters.

We heard a whistle. The Ukrainians jumped into the open cars. They were there to keep us safe so that God forbid, nothing bad should happen to us…they too, were there to protect us!

The train started moving, in the direction of Ponary. My heart was pounding with fear. Perhaps it was already here? But no. There, we were past Ponary. The train moved along to Landwarów, later to become known as Lentvaris. Before we entered the Landwarów station, they closed the shutters of the hatch above. We were left sitting in the dark. There was no air to breathe. We were suffocating, praying for death to come already. The train ran on and on. *Could we be going straight to Treblinka?*

It finally stopped. They opened the shutters. The train was standing in the middle of a field, with nothing around us. The Ukrainians jumped out and came into the cars. Three entered my car and demanded "hush money." A lot of money. Otherwise, our fate would be bad and bitter. Between us, we collected the money and gave it to them. They needed women's wristwatches, too, and they were given a few. In exchange, they promised not to close the windows. We stood in the field until evening.

I continued to weave a plan to escape, by jumping through the hatch. I would follow the sages' advice and distance myself from them. Perhaps…the nights were very dark and when the train was running, the executioners sat in their huts. And anyway, what did I have to lose? We went through Grodno. It was the way to Treblinka.

I imagined myself jumping off the train. I knew what was waiting for me. But again, I wasn't that afraid of death. Still, maybe I was meant to stay alive.

I felt like telling someone about it. A woman I knew was standing in front of me. Doctor Sadlas, from Vilnius. She was in her white coat, as they had taken her from the hospital. She had no coat, no bundle to sit on. She stood leaning against the wall. I told her about my plan and decision. She looked at me sadly, envying my daring, my decisiveness. But she couldn't do it. I didn't try to convince her to. It was certainly a bold step, but it was better to die a bold death than a sheep's death. Tears rolled from her eyes. I prepared my basket with a few slices of bread and a number of small items. I tied everything in a white handkerchief, so that if I survived, I would be able to find it in the dark.

7

The train continued on its way. We passed through the Rūdiškės Station in the dark, so that the esteemed locals wouldn't see the train with its very important passengers...

We traveled on. It was dim and dark outside, and it was dim and dark inside. The people in the car slowly fell silent and dozed off. They even slept standing up. Some talked in their sleep, crying and moaning. One elderly woman was talking in her sleep about her dead husband. She was complaining to him for leaving her on her own to be tortured. I remembered the old doctor in Vilnius, Dr. Gershoni. When his wife died in the ghetto, he committed suicide. "Why should she sit all on her own up in heaven, while I am suffering in the hell here, down below?" they say were his last words before he died.

I stood on my bundle facing the hatch. There was only one idea running about inside my head now: *I will not blindly follow Hitlers orders. No! After all, my son, too is of the same opinion. I am tearing the evil order of that devil with my own two hands. One more moment - and it will happen. This is the way and there is no stopping me.*

Time passed. I thought that I might miss my moment. I listened to the wheels clattering. I had nothing more to wait for. *God!* I woke up the dozing doctor and asked her to give me a little help, because the hatch was slightly too high. I offered her my bundle of belongings. It included a coat that she could wear.

I threw my basket out and listened closely. It was quiet now. The doctor helped me. She reminded me that I had to jump forward, in the direction the train was traveling in; and to push myself as far away as possible from the cars. I knew that. I crawled through the hatch, still holding myself with one hand. I made sure to whisper: *Death to Hitler!* I let go - and was out.

I lay strewn on the ground. The 54 cars, jammed full of people traveling toward their death, passed me by. The train disappeared. I was left on my own. I was alive. There was rustling in my head. My face was wet with blood. I didn't know quite what was hurting. My hands were fine. My legs were fine. I quickly jumped to my feet, but I wavered, groggy, but not from wine. I wiped my face and spat a few teeth out of my mouth. Around me, it was pitch black, and there was a frightening kind of silence.

I ran back along the tracks, looking for my basket. I ran a long way, but there it was, shining white in the dark. I quickly got off the railroad tracks, out of the trains' way. I lay down under a tree, breathing heavily, but not because I was very weak. I thought that even if they shot me now, I wouldn't move from my spot.

Suddenly, a German guard appeared nearby me. They were patrolling with flashlights in their hands and checking the way, checking the tracks. I lay where I was like the living dead. Luckily, they didn't have a dog. They were walking slowly. They passed by and continued on their way. I could no longer see them. I knew that I had to run on. I had to get away from where I was, and fast. It was dangerous by the railroad tracks. I could see a dark spot in the distance. Was it a hay stack or logs for a bonfire? I crawled closer to the spot. There were a few logs, but at some distance from the railway tracks. I sat down, praying to God that the night would never end. Danger would return again when day broke. I had no one and nowhere to go. But my thoughts passed quickly to those being transported on the train. Would any of them survive, would any of them return?

I tried to understand the way those Germans were thinking: Why, in fact, were they killing the Jewish people? Perhaps it was to incriminate the entire world along with them, for its silence? And perhaps they were playing a game, a "trading" game with the Western world, with the Allies - "Take the live Jews if you want to save them, and give us…what?"

Night passed slowly, evading something that would eventually overcome it. Like my passing thoughts - changing. Dawn was already turning the sky gray. I took out a small mirror. I had a wound near my temple. Nonsense! I took stock: I had to be alert now, in every sense. I turned to go another way. A side way.

I didn't really have a Jewish appearance. I was dressed like a regular woman, with a gray basket from rough fabric in my hand. There were just a few teeth missing…it was me.

I didn't know the area and I didn't know where I was. But I knew that I had to get as far away as possible from where I was. I passed through the woods. Some were smaller, others bigger. There were a few lone houses scattered on the steppe. On the horizon, villages appeared, farms, intermingled with the woods. After them, the closer I got - there was forest. Forest, all around - forest. I came across water. I washed myself, cleaned what I still had in my possession. I wanted to look like a human being, like a regular woman, so that they wouldn't recognize where I came from on me, and where…

(After the liberation, when I returned to Vilnius, I met Mrs. Trok there. She was also from Vilnius. She had been imprisoned in the same car as me. She, too, had managed to escape, two days after me. She told me that they left the ill and the children on their own in Treblinka. From there, the entire convoy headed for Lublin. Probably to Majdanek, from where no one returned.)

8

I decided to walk until the forest, and if I hurried, I'd have a chance to get there without running into anyone. In the past few years, I'd learned to be very careful. I walked, comparing myself as a hunted animal. The comparison was seemingly unnecessary.

I breathed a sigh of relief when I reached the forest without being noticed. The forest was thick, with mostly trees and shrubs. It was as big as the sea. Or as the desert - for me. And who was I supposed to meet there? I thought that it would have been good if I could stay there for a while, until I had investigated and learned the area; perhaps found a sign of the partisans from Vilnius.

It was an extremely ancient forest. Thousands of years old, I guessed. It sprawled over dozens of square miles full of marshes, mountains, and hills and valleys, across the width and breadth. Villages sprouted on its edges, expansive and widespread. Others were smaller in area and seemed to have been tucked away by force into that jungle.

I'd been sitting like next to a thick bush for hours. It hid me completely. Dusk came, and darkness fell on the forest. I headed toward a house that I'd earmarked beforehand. After all, the choice was mine! What would all the people in the *malina* have had to say about it? A big dog lay in the doorway. And wonders of wonders: He didn't bark at all. He even looked at me with friendly eyes, as if inviting me in.

Inside, I was met by an aging Christian man and his wife of the same age. They were amazed that their dog had allowed me in without barking even once. By nature, he was very irritable.

I told them that I was on my way to Grodno. I was walking there. It was hard now to get where you wanted to go by car. And as we were talking about this and that, I proposed to them - since I wasn't in any hurry to get there, and I could see that they were digging up potatoes - as such, if they wished, I was willing to help them with the work, and only then to continue to Grodno. My suggestion sounded good to them and they welcomed me with open joy, as if they'd known me for years. Things for her, the housewife, really were hard without help. Their only help was their daughter, and she was just 15. Their potatoes had done very well that year, and they had a big crop. Enough for an entire year for them, their animals and even to share. Then she asked me about papers. It was evening, and for the time being, I could stay with them. After all, they didn't know me. I got a bad and bitter feeling in my heart. Talk, I couldn't, and there was no point in keeping silent. After some hesitation, I decided to tell them my sad story, including of my escape. I had no papers, nor money or valuables.

They were stunned that I'd remained healthy and in one piece. And at my chase after my basket. I should know, they told me, that landmines blew up night and day on and beside the tracks where I'd run the day before. The partisans would plant landmines there before a train arrived. Precisely the night before, they didn't. Amazing. A true miracle from heaven. Perhaps I was a righteous woman.

They would look into the situation within a few days. In the end, those were crazy days. They had to discuss it. They had other children, older, and another family living with them, too. The family was away visiting relatives. I was to spend the night in the granary.

The following morning, I would go out to dig up potatoes. I was to be very careful of the shepherd, they warned me. He hated Jews.

I ate a bowl of potato soup with bread and went straight to the granary, to sleep. The granary was big and half was full with hay. The warm soup had refreshed me a little after many hungry days.

I made a place for myself in the hay. Flies and mosquitoes try to bite me, but apparently, I wasn't to their liking. I was too skinny, and probably too salty. In the ghetto, we were still able somehow to get hold of a little salt, and we used it instead of sugar. Or maybe they were Aryan mosquitoes and I wasn't good enough for them. Thank you very much. I willingly forewent their friendship. Either way, I rested well. On my part, the night could have gone on forever. I fell asleep quickly and dreamed of strange things. The dream seemed to be predicting better days. Was that so?

In the morning I was already in the yard. The shepherd narrowed one eye at me. I had to be very careful of him. He gathered the animals and I wouldn't see him again until evening. I walked right into the house. There were already people there. They were all members of the household. Two sons and a daughter. They gave me a quick breakfast, a bowl of soup and bread, and the daughter went with me to the field to dig up potatoes.

On the first day, I found the work very difficult. I had grown weak and my hands trembled. But I continued without saying a word, as I had to prove myself. It was my only means of rescue. In the middle of work, the neighboring women came to see the new potato digger.

My "Pani," Lapinska was her name, was also among the visitors. I heard her explaining: I was from the city. From Grodno. I worked slowly, but cleanly. I didn't require supervision.

It was my first test in the potato field. That night, too, I slept on the threshing floor and went to work again the following morning.

The other family returned. The head of the family was a high-ranking, Polish official. He was unemployed and had a wife and two children, a boy of 10 and a boy of 12. They were refugees from Galicia, which once belonged to Austria. They also spoke beautiful German. They discussed me, and decided that I'd continue to work and sleep in the granary for the meanwhile. They'd see what day would bring.

They were two families, altogether nine people, and they were risking themselves for me. There were still other kinds of people, human beings, in the world.

I dug up potatoes for the Lapinski family for over a month. They got used to me and trusted me. I had passed the test. Other residents of the village were jealous of my Lapinskis, for finding such good help.

The potato season was over. I couldn't continue to sleep in the granary. The cold days had begun, and also because of the surrounding neighbors, who we couldn't allow to suspect that I was hiding.

The two families, the Lapinskis and the Lankas (the refugee family) again discussed what to do with me. They were afraid to keep me in the house. They didn't want to tell me to leave, They may have been influenced by the fact that the Red Army was already fighting on the border and on Polish soil. And when the Reds arrived, it wouldn't do them any harm to have saved a Jewish woman.

I knew perfectly well that I had nowhere to go, no one to turn to. I still didn't know the way to the Vilnius partisans and they were far away. Nothing had changed yet. There was still nothing new under the sun.

There was an incident, and Pan Lanka found a job in the Kaunas area and left for a long time. Only then did I leave the granary. Pani Lanka welcomed me into her room. I slept in a good bed, with clean, white linen.

That's how I became part the Lapinski household. They were religious, devoted people who proved themselves to be truly decent.

I lived with these families for a whole six months that included many difficult days and sleepless nights, for me and for my protectors. Lapinski would repeatedly say, perhaps to reassure himself, that no one would imagine he was keeping a Jewish woman in his home, right under the nose of the German and Lithuanian police. He spoke excellent Lithuanian, and when the Lithuanian police sometimes came to visit, he would talk to them. Pani Lanka would talk to the Germans.

The Lanka family's financial situation was dire. The Lapinskis took them in, gave them a room to live in, and helped them as much as they could. But their ability to help was rather limited. They, too, often had nothing to eat. Food shortages at the time were a problem for many. They had a plenty of land, but it was mostly sandy and poor. They also lacked farmhands. Their eldest son was sick. The youngest was healthy and a "hero" and he attended university. He refused to stay in the village. His mother, Pani Lapinska was a country woman, and used to talk about him as "My pan agronomist." The old couple themselves and their younger daughter did all the work. Luckily, their potato crop was good that year, and there was also no shortage of milk for the soup. That's what they ate three times a day, in various forms. And often, when Pani Lanka had nothing to cook, she, too, would come to the table and have potato soup, with her children.

Pan Lapinski and Pani Lanka would travel often to the Rūdiškės train station. The train station served in those days as a center for all the news in the vicinity. Sometimes, they would bring back a newspaper and news from other sources, not from the newspaper. That news was different, and calming and claimed, among other things, that the Red Army was advancing and that the Germans were retreating and fleeing "in exemplary order." My heart pounding, I would listen to the secret conversations about Jewish and non-Jewish partisans in the steppe and forests of Rūdiškės. They were spotted once in the village, and again in another village. Here they blew up a bridge, and there, they delayed a train or dismantled the railroad tracks for miles. And in some unidentified place, Germans had been killed. And almost every evening, a landmine would explode, even under the trains themselves.

The Germans wised up. The front cars would be left empty, and when they flew into the air, they would clear the way, replace the train tracks, which they always brought with them, and the train would continue on its way. But the partisans didn't let up. They laid the landmines in such a way that they blew up under the middle of the train, or under the locomotive. I often saw a train running with its cars on fire. The luminance was spectacular.

The Germans reduced the trains running through those areas to a minimum. They also tried to cut down the trees along the railway tracks, so that the partisans couldn't reach their target without being seen. But the partisans stubbornly and enthusiastically continued, although with more casualties of their own.

How many partisans fell in that way? One unfortunate Jewish partisan lost both of his legs while performing his mission. The Lithuanian police brought him to Rūdiškės. He begged them to shoot him, but the dogs tortured him until he passed away. There were other, similar incidences. They were heartbreaking. I would be horrified whenever I heard such news. Only God knew if my children were still alive.

Mother! And if indeed, they were still alive, where were they? And many other children of other moms and dads. So many wonderful young people and youths fled to the forests to fight against the enemy. My heart went out to the partisans. I wanted to meet them, but they were not at all eager to meet me, it seemed. The partisans needed young fighters. In any case, they hadn't been seen for a long time in those places. They must have had other, more important strategic targets. And indeed, they were active on the other side of the steppe There were Jews from Lithuania with them, who had fled Hitler's regime, and Russians, too, Red Army soldiers who had escaped from German captivity.

9

Staying with the Lapinskis had become more problematic. In winter, the farmers had more free time. With more time on their hands, they would go to visit each other. Visitors came to the Lapinskis from other villages, too. To them, I was a friend of Pani Lanka, and I was always busy with something in her room. Pani Lanka was considered by them to be an authority and she did not have to report to anyone on her friends and acquaintances.

There were various guests. One of them, with pretentions of being an advocate by education, would kiss the ladies' hands in greeting, like the Polish, while carefully probing them. An advocate or not? His favorite subject was - the Jews. In fact, he would have hanged them all. Shot them, burned them. Yes, as a true and devoted Polish man, he would never forgive the Germans for invading Poland, but for one thing he was grateful to them - for releasing Poland from the Jews. What an ingenious operation!

Guests also came from across the Polish border - from Lithuania. There, the Jewish partisans had good acquaintances and often, when necessary, they would spend the night with them.

The Lapinskis' friend from the town of Trakai, 15 miles from Vilnius, was also a frequent visitor. The area around Trakai was very beautiful. The scenery there was wonderful and there was something to see. It was also surrounded by streams and springs. In "primordial" years, Trakai served as an attraction and place to travel during the summer months for the youth of Vilnius. They nicknamed it "Venice." Before the war, the town was populated by Polish, Lithuanian, Jews and many Karaites.

The man from Trakai, had a lot of time to look and listen. And he, too, was able to tell us how the Germans and the Lithuanian police had jointly murdered the Jews of Trakai, and the Jews everywhere in the vicinity.

It was the fall of 1941. All the Jews had been gathered together from the towns, villages and communities around, and from Rūdiškės and Landwaro, too. They were transported, the big and the small, the young and the old, to Trakai, while they were told that a ghetto had been built for them, where they would put all the Jews of the area. It was a bold-faced lie. In Trakai, the beautiful Venice of Lithuania, they were murdering everyone using a variety of strange methods that the murderers could come up with, in order to exterminate the many thousands of Jews. They were sentenced to fire and water and submachine guns and machine guns.

All the Jews of the towns and villages around Vilnius, and from all the suburbs of the city, were similarly murdered. The Jews from many of the towns and villages further away were concentrated together and murdered in the fields of the Yashoni district. Here, the Jews of Turgelis, Leipiskis and Trav perished.

Not all of the victims went like sheep to the slaughter. Many of the Jews who were deceived tried to rebel; to resist. They were the first to be shot, some of them on the spot.

Pani Lapinska told me about a wealthy Jewish woman from Rūdiškės, A. Mosmanova, who, not long before the war, prevented her only son from going to Palestine, even though he already had all of the necessary papers. She couldn't understand how one could leave a wealthy, established home to go starve on some kibbutz, even if it was in the Land of Israel. The end, of course, was the same end of all the Jews. Overnight, a torrential wind swept away and eradicated the entire, affluent house, which had been built in the sand. The woman, along with her son was shot dead by the edge of that same mass pit.

And Pani Lapinska had more stories: Once, on a stormy, raining night, back in 1941, someone knocked on their window. They went out to the stranger. It was a young man, who instead of a coat, was wrapped in the parchment of a Torah scroll. He'd walked from Kaunas, from the Yeshiva in Slobodka, and he was trying to get to the city of Mir, in White Russia. He asked for a slice of bread and a place to spend the night. They gave him bread, but they were afraid of allowing him to sleep there. I understood that he was from Mir and had attended the Yeshiva in Slobodka. I wonder if he ever arrived at his destination.

I heard many, more similar sad stories in the Lapinski home, in those dark days. The soil in the Vilnius area was fertilized and fattened by Jewish blood. Jews who tried to save themselves, ran from the fire into the water, in the fields, in the forests, on difficult routes and via every lane and path. They perished from starvation, from the cold, and at the hands of human animals who received hush money for their heads.

The Jews were outlawed. They lacked human rights and

protection. Moreover: Anyone who robbed and murdered a Jew received credit for doing so, and the more the better. At times, things went so far as to award a decoration of excellence for "fighting against the enemy."

One day, a rumor spread that the Red Army had broken through the enemy's flanks and was already fighting on Polish soil. Because they had conquered the cities Rovno, Brest- Litovsk, and many other towns and cities. Everyone believed that soon the heroic Red Army would get there. But there is a vast difference between talk and taking action. It wasn't like the beginning of the "miracle" of the summer of 1920, when Budyonny and his cavalry withdrew the Polish legionaries from Smolensk, straight to Warsaw.

I recall, and I would like to mention here a few lines from the Yiddish poem by Shalom Zichman, who was a young Jewish poet living at the time in Vilnius. (The Red Army released him in 1930 from the Biaroza-Kartuzskaya prison):

Like a flash in front of my eyes,
The cavalry galloped
And Budyonny flew at the lead.

After that, came the pan, loping
Stealing youth and freedom.

And with the spark of life in my gut
Barely still whispering, burning
I will still see him before me
Budyonny, flying, galloping.

The Budyonnys of our time did not fly. They advanced while involved in heavy combat with the well-fortified enemy, protected by iron and steel. And in order to melt that iron and steel, the Budyonnys of our times needed immeasurably powerful fire. And indeed, their guns thundered day and night, their tanks and Katyusha rockets spitting fire…

One day, we noticed that the Germans were retreating in our area, too. They destroyed everything in their way, leaving scorched earth in the cities, towns and villages. And the people? Some were shot, others were hanged, and others were taken along with them. On the road leading to Leningrad, the soldiers of the Red Army came across avenues of gallows, with the bodies of Russian civilians swinging in the wind.

On one freezing day in January, a long train full of refugees from Vitebsk, a city in the north of White Russia, stopped at the Rūdiškės train station. They were mostly women and children. They were held in the cars for two days. Then the peasants from the vicinity were given permission to host the refugees in their homes, if they so wished.

Immediately, peasants began arriving from towns and villages near and far. Polish and Lithuanian people registered and took with them entire families to host. There was enough work on the farms for everyone. "My" farm also hosted refugees. Three families, who "passed on regards" to me from the Jews of Vitebsk. "There were many Jews there, and suddenly, there are no more," in that style. The Germans also drowned many of them in the river there. "Fish also want to live," their joke spread about the village. That was what happened to the

Jews of Vitebsk, Marc Chagall's town.

The arrival of refugees in the area made my stay with the Lapinskis much easier. There were so many new faces to see that they were no longer looked at. The refugees, however, had papers, while I had none.

But it did become easier to breathe. The Lithuanian Guard, who had taken over the beautiful hunting palace, were chased away. Before the war, the Polish government ministers invited someone they considered to be important, the German minister Göring, to hunt on the steppe and in the lush forests.

There were now no animals again on the Rudniki steppe. It is hard to say whether Göring had managed to shoot them all, or if they simply chased two or three pigs belonging to the peasants and gave them the appearance of wild pigs, to make their most respectful guest happy…

The partisan ranks had grown stronger and they set up scout guards on the edges of the forests. Their activities were also more dangerous now, and bolder. People said that they had received fighters and the most advanced equipment and hand weapons as reinforcement.

Often, in the quiet evenings, a Soviet aircraft would fly low toward the steppe. We could recognize it by its special buzz.

10

A new element entered the picture: Akubazs, the Armia Krajowa (the Home Army). Others called them the "White Poles." Those were Gangs from the Armia Krajowa put themselves at the Gestapo's disposal. They received full gear, weapons and cars. And they took it upon themselves to wipe out the Red partisans on the Rudniki steppe. They were looking for Jewish partisans in particular. The Red Army was advancing and getting closer, and they were concerned that the Germans would not manage to wipe out all of the Jews in the forests. In short, they were there to "kill Jews and save Poland," as the well-known slogan said. This job seemed to be made especially for them. Until then, they'd been running rampant in Polish territories. Now, they were popping up where we were, too. They also now had the opportunity to take revenge on the Lithuanians, to settle accounts, from time immemorial. They murdered a number of Lithuanians, set fire to some of their farms, and declared holy war on the Red partisans. They also organized the Polish youth in the villages to join the fight. The situation for the partisans on the other side of the steppe grew much worse, as they never knew who was with them and who was against them; who was friend and who was foe. But this deployment did not yet interfere with most of the partisan activities and targets.

The railroads and so on, important factories and fortifications, were on Lithuanian soil.

11

Winter was coming to an end and a visitor arrived. Pan Lanka came for a few days. He was working as a bookkeeper at a sawmill in the vicinity of Kaunas. The sawmill manager, a German from Danzig, thought that Lanka was German, and he spouted a variety of intimate ideas to him. Among other things, Lanka asked him what he thought of the rapid progress of the Red Army. To that, the German answered that he'd stopped thinking. All he knew was that he was better off today than he would be tomorrow. Another time, Lanka asked for his opinion on the extermination of the Jews. To that the manager replied that he, a trader from Danzig, had been in the trading business with Jewish forest traders for years, and they were most certainly decent people. But he believed that Hitler had a better understanding of Jewish affairs than he did.

Lanka also said that, not far from the sawmill, 40 Jews were working on road repairs. They had all run away just a few days earlier, probably to join the partisans in the forests. He also brought with him a lot of German newspapers, old and new. One newspaper happily informed its readers that

Hungary, too, had finally started to exterminate the Jews. As if the murder of a million Hungarian Jews would bring salvation and redemption for the already rocky Third Reich, because if Hungary did what Berlin wanted, it was a sign that the thousand-year-old Reich was indeed guaranteed.

An even more dated illustrated weekly told, in pictures, of the successful conquest of the Russian port Sevastopol by the Black Sea, as well as pictures of the occupied city of Stalingrad. As it turned out later, the Germans were too quick to make their official announcements.

I picked up the German newspaper, the Völkischer Beobachter, from recent days. On the first page, there was an article by Goebbels, under a bold-lettered heading: "The Jews will not celebrate a new Purim holiday again." In his article, Goebbels poured derision and libel on the Jews, who because of their fake stories, the poor innocent vizier Haman was hanged from a tree. That article appeared on the eve of Purim, 1944. I read it with the joy of revenge, thinking, *Yes, so it was, you murderers! You recalled the evil Haman's end. We can see your guilt on you, you criminals, the kind of which the world has not yet known. I doubt that I would ever get to see it, but you, too, will be hanged, of that I am sure.*

The burning gunpowder coming from every direction hung in the air. The Russian cargo planes and heavy bombers loaded with bombs passed over our heads making powerful booms, , sliced through the air. They were hurrying to the front. They were pressed for time. Part of the German army was stuck there like in a sack.

The Polish servants of the Gestapo had attacked a Russian family in Rūdiškės. They had been living there for a long time. They took three men out onto the street and shot them for no reason at all. A bitter commotion broke out among the refugees from Viciebsk. Many fled to the forests, to the Red partisans. A lot of Lithuanian peasants had already fled deep into the forests.

One day, a neighbor brought news from Vilnius. He'd seen Jewish children and women being led to a train. It was March 27, 1944. The German murderers had pulled the children from their parents' arms, the Jews of Vilnius who were still living in the Kailis and HKP forced labor camps.

The ruler of Rūdiškės in those days, a Dutch Nazi, made threats of using the *zonder* polizei, who would release a torrent of bombs from above on the Red partisans, which he indeed tried to do. But despite all the threats, the partisan ranks grew from day to day. A new company of partisans from White Russia arrived as reinforcements. "The Mobile Company." They acted as pioneers and advanced before the Red Army, through fields and swamps, continually hounding the enemy. They were called the Morosovchis, after their commander, Morosov.

The bombing of the partisans in the forests did not bear fruit and the partisans continued doing their thing. The German then implemented another ploy against them: total siege, in order to starve them. They blocked all the roads and paths leading to the steppe forests. To this end, they enlisted the Polish youths from the villages, who were delighted with the honorable they'd been assigned.

Within all that turmoil, two "novel" Jewish tragedies shocked me. Some say that every person is an entire world. If so, then two worlds were destroyed.

A young Jewish man from Vilnius, by the name of Rodnitzky, lived as an Aryan, with documents. For quite some time, he had been working as a foreman in a turpentine factory. Danger was lurking, but liberation was imminent. As it happened, he went to the Ministry of Labor in Trakai to take care of something for the laborers. A woman from Vilnius recognized him there and informed on him. He was a musician, a Jew from Vilnius. He was immediately arrested. His world collapsed on him. He was shot in Trakai, in the heart of Lithuanian Venice.

The Christians in the vicinity had different views on the matter. Some were very upset by the Jewish audacity; to deceive the ruling Germans and their Lithuanian police! Others were most surprised by the Jewish bravery.

The second victim was a Jewish man of about 30, 35, from Rūdiškės. The Lithuanian police arrested him in the garden of a village peasant. His sentence was sealed on the spot. He was shot in the Rūdiškės cemetery. The farmer was also arrested. He paid a ransom of a large pig and a small barrel of schnapps. They produced schnapps on a large scale in the towns and villages in the region.

My Lapinskis and also Pani Lanka were extremely perplexed and frightened by the latter incident. They were afraid to let me stay at home. Nine people didn't have to suffer because of me. Granted, they knew full well that I had nowhere to go, but they could no longer help me. First and foremost, a person is committed to themselves and to their families. Pani Lanka was particularly afraid. She dreamed that dogs had bitten her so badly that her boys didn't recognize her.

I understood them, I truly did. Seemingly, they were certainly right. They had enough concerns of their own. Health concerns, family issues, and many financial worries that every farmer had from the dawn of his youth to the grave. As such, they didn't lack for concerns other than for me. I knew very clearly that I had to leave. To distance myself.

Everything was good and fine, in accordance with justice and honesty and sound logic. But where was I to go? To whom? Did I have anyone else in the world? A place to lay my head?

The world was big, but for me, a Jewish woman, my circle was extremely limited. If I protected my head - my legs would be in danger. Who would protect my head? That was not just a picturesque parable. It was reality, in itself.

My only possible route led to the partisans on the steppe. I hoped there was a place for me among them. But the steppe was so big and expansive, and intimidating, and they are hard to get to. All of the roads leading to the partisan camps in the forests were strictly guarded, with no one coming or going. After all, the Germans had decided to starve them to death under siege, like the siege of the Babylonians and the Assyrians and the Greeks and the Romans of the ancient world.

12

One spring morning in April, I left the Lapinskis. I thanked them for the great deal of good that they did me, took my bundle - the basket and a slice of bread - and began a new chapter in my wandering path through life.

I went to the forests, to the partisans, slipping through difficult routes, forcing myself to be wary of the people I knew, too, so that they wouldn't notice where I was going. There were those who considered the partisans to be people from another world, who caused trouble and nothing else. I skipped over potholes and bushes, through the trees and the stones. The route was longer, but a little safer. Again, I saw myself as a hunted doe.

Eventually I got there. It appeared to be the right forest. I tried to go deeper into the forest. The prevailing silence there scared me, as did the grim, thick, dense trees. There was a stack of chopped firewood there, probably from a few years back. I built myself a hiding place among the wooden planks, hidden from view from all sides. I sat inside and watched out for my partisans to arrive.

I could see a very narrow path, not far away. People probably passed by there, I thought. Everything around was imbued with disorder. In fact, it wasn't really a forest, but a true steppe, full of hills and ditches with wild vegetation.

The day passed and no one showed up. Not even one, single partisan. I was struck by fear. I left my hiding place and returned to the edge of the forest. At dusk, I found myself in a meadow among low trees. There, I spent the night, which was different from all other nights. Bone-penetrating cold and fear and horror. And the dark trees, in the image and form of the angel of death, leaned over me. The steppe seemed to come alive at night. It filled with strange sounds and voices; running around, bouncing and skipping. I realized that these were forest animals in their home. Someone had misled me a few days ago: There were indeed still animals there. The night was as long as a thousand years. It went on and on. My teeth chattered. I stayed a "little" longer like that, another day and night.

In the afternoon, I noticed three partisans moving along a side path. They were armed with machine guns. I ran and caught up with them. They were very puzzled, meeting someone there, in the clearing in the steppe woods. The three were Lithuanians.

I introduced myself to them, telling them briefly about my short pedigree, about my path, paved with thorns, and I asked them to help me find the Vilnius partisan camp there, in the steppe. One of them said, "You do speak beautifully, but nice things alone will not help you. You're a spy. A German emissary, or you've been sent by the White Poles." I wouldn't come out of this alive, I thought, thinking that they would shoot me. I protested emphatically: "How can a persecuted Jew like me be a spy for the Nazis?" I begged them to take me to their commander.

"But you aren't at all Jewish," they said. They checked every little thing of mine, every piece of fabric, each one giving me a different examination. One of them examined me in spoken and written Yiddish. My examiner, who gave the impression of being an educated man, whispered with the other two. They led me deeper into the forest, to the guard's hut. There, they locked me up and left. I remained alone. The thought of them thinking that I was a spy sent by the Germans gave me no respite. It was annoying. Me - a spy! It would have been hilarious if it wasn't so tragic. Although I didn't have a Jewish nose, but didn't my eyes, Jewish and sad, say it all? Was it not evident from what I said that I was truly a Jewish woman, a living miracle? Many hours passed by like that. I was left to my thoughts until I stopped thinking entirely, pinning my hopes on God and on people - the partisans.

The partisans arrived, two from before and the third - a man from Kaunas. The latter interrogated me on many matters. He had relatives and acquaintances In Vilnius. In the end, he determined that I was indeed a Jew from Vilnius, and that I wasn't a spy. And regarding the partisans from Vilnius - he gave me no hint. "Perhaps I could spend some time in your camp?" I asked.

"That is out of the question," he said. Anyway, I wasn't to ask them for anything. I couldn't return to the forest, as I could be shot. The partisans lived by their own laws. Their lives were tough, and so were their laws. I was also to forget that I'd been with them. Then they took me out of the forest - and disappeared. I stood in the road leading to a large village. Logic dictated that I couldn't go there. Danger was lurking for me in every house. It began to grow dark. Maybe the peasants were busy now, I thought. There was the village which I have left. I took my life into my own hands and walked through the length of the village. I walked to the Lapinskis, thinking that perhaps they would take me in as a guest for the night. The next day, early in the morning, I would head for the other side of the steppe. Perhaps luck would shine on me there.

The Lapinskis were not very happy to see me. But as I was already there…the next day they were starting to plant potatoes, if I wanted to help…I helped to prepare and to select. Pani Lanka and the children completed the group. A few other girls, neighbors, joined us. The company became noisy and cheerful.

The planted field was not far from the steppe; from the forest. After a few hours of work, German planes flew over our heads. Heavy bombers. They flew straight over the partisans. A moment later - and the bombs roared across the forest. The ground tremored beneath us. All of a sudden, we were being shot at from all sides. We all lay close to the ground. The shooters from above probably believed that they'd been lucky and that they'd taken out a whole gang of "bandits." But we were also lucky. When they stopped shooting, we got to our feet, all of us healthy and in one piece. No one was injured. Some of us examined every part of their body. The situation was like a tragicomedy that could have turned out differently. The trees near us took most of the bullets. They were stuck in them. "This is my exchange, this is my substitute, this is my atonement," I recalled the Yom Kippur prayer. Thick smoke rose from the partisans' forest, billowing into space above. We quickly finished the job, and wary and afraid, returned home.

I spent a few more days with the Lapinskis. There was no lack of work on the farm during the spring season. I worked planting tobacco. The soil there was good for such crops. And I was already an expert in the field.

At the time, the situation of the partisans who were operating in that region greatly deteriorated. All the routes out were barricaded. The Germans, Lithuanians, the Akubazs and even the Ukrainians who popped up from somewhere, were enlisted for a confrontation with the partisans. A confrontation of bloodshed. The partisans looked for new ways to break the siege.

Once, at midnight on a quiet night, we suddenly heard barrages of shots at one end of town. I dressed in an instant. The house woke up with a start, but we spoke in whispers. We didn't turn on the light. Even the dog, who had recently been kept in the corridor of the house at night, was held firmly so that it wouldn't bark.

And then we heard noise. People running, moving, horses, carts, bombs exploding around the Lapinskis' garden and house. A partisan company had snuck past the railroad tracks, which were guarded day and night. In order to draw the attention of the Guard Corps to other direction, they set up a machine gun at one end of the village and began firing without interruption, and so they were able to break the siege and return to their forest.

The deceived Germans sought to absolve themselves. A number of armored vehicles came from the nearest train station and started to shower the village with bullets. The partisans were already out of their range.

Bullets hit the neighbor's house and the owner was injured. The Germans were already in the village, looking for partisans, checking and identifying residents. I was redundant there, I had to escape quickly. I slipped away by the cowsheds and into the woods. There, I waited for the light of day. In that area, the houses and fields seemed tucked between the small woods.

In the morning, I continued on my way. To the partisans! The steppe was infinitely huge. I went in a different direction than the time before. I prayed in my heart that I wouldn't run into the Lithuanian partisans again. I had with me my constant partner, my little basket. In order to distract the attention of the all-seeing from me, I knelt down and gathered small spring mushrooms. I had to be very careful of the shepherds, too, who always saw more than they should. Now my path led me to a larger village. The Lapiskis' dog got me there. He jumped on me and barked with joy for finding me.

The good, faithful dog! He'd warned me of danger several times before, by barking. Oh, if only people were dogs like him! How good it would be to live in the world…but what would I do now! I couldn't go with him; the Lapiskis would never forgive me if he got lost. I had to go back and return their dog. They immediately tied him up with a rope, so that he wouldn't run after me. I told Pani Lanka which village I was about to enter, and she gripped her head with both hands and made the sign of a cross. That was where all the kidnappers of Jews were lurking for prey like me

13

Once again, I went wandering about, through fields and forests and clearings, until I arrived at the edge of the partisans' forest. I walked east along the edge. I had not yet lost hope of meeting someone from Vilnius. Along the way, I bypassed the villages that went deeper into the steppe. And so, while I was walking, I found myself in a marshy area. The mosquitoes bit me and drew blood. I expected to have difficulty getting out of the mud, so I returned to dryer land. I didn't see any houses around. It started to rain. Everything around me was wet. I found a hiding place under a fir tree with branches that tilted down, like a kind of umbrella.

It rained for two days and two nights. All that time, I sat under the tree like an Indian fakir, leaning against its friendly trunk. Oh, if people were only as friendly as that tree! I became completely silent paralyzed. My only companion was my mute hand basket, on which I sat, soaking wet.

But it didn't rain forever, and eventually, it stopped. Spring arrived and the sun was shining. It began to warm up and I crawled out from between the gray branches. At first, I stood like a pole, barely moving my legs. Then I sat in the sun, rubbing my legs and my entire body, and wrung and dried my things out. I slowly started to become a little human again. I washed a little in a nearby stream and put my hair and limbs into a semblance of order. I couldn't continue sitting there. There was no point.

I likened sitting under that tree for those two days and two nights to sitting inside a grave. The strange silence also seemed to me to be of that world. As such, I dashed off, trying to walk on dryer terrain, and onward, in search of people. I hadn't found the Vilnius partisans, and I knew that I may possibly never find them. Therefore, I turned to those who I did meet. I went into a house nearby the forest and bought bread from the people there, who looked at me suspiciously. I was a stranger in the area, not a local. They sold me the bread with blatant reluctance. Then I returned to the forest to look for the partisans again. I carefully checked all the roads and trails leading to the forests I stopped by a wider road and tried to walk along it. I noticed people's footprints, but they were immediately swallowed up by the grass. Then I stopped. There was a fence in front of me.

Piled up there, were uprooted and broken trees. Some were twisted, as if they'd been hit by lightning. A little further on, there were more fences, some that seemed to have popped up on their own, as if naturally, and others put there by man. I remembered that someone at the Lapinskis told me that the partisans had planted landmines along all the routes leading deeper into the forest. I wasn't, heaven forbid, complaining about them. After all, they weren't aiming at someone like me. I found a side path and proceeded with caution. And so,

I landed up at a partisan lookout point. There, I luckily ran into a Jewish partisan from one of the Jewish villages. He was somewhat puzzled and a little encouraged himself. I told him about my troubles, about myself and what I was looking for. Okay, he said, he would report to the commander. He asked me if I had any bread with me. They had run out at the camp few days earlier. I gave him my bread.

Soon the guard would be changing, he told me, he would report me, hand his rifle over and leave. I was to stay there and wait. Later, another one came and I went with him to the commander.

The commander, a former Russian officer, received me and was friendly, but with the same friendliness, denied my request. They had no way of incorporating women. They needed men. Fighters. They were facing a tough and decisive battle with the retreating Germans, and with their many, various assistants. The road to Grodno passed between them and the Vilnius partisans, who were being closely guarded by the Germans. I couldn't get there. There was, however, another way there, for someone who knew the route well; through the swamps, which were about twelve miles in length. He said a friendly goodbye to me and warned me not to roam about the partisan forests again, because they'd shoot me without "Pardon". That is, without even asking for forgiveness. They escorted me out of the forest along another route and pointed out a small village through which I could pass. Again, I remained alone on the edge of the forest.

And again, I had nowhere to go. And again, I slept under a tree that night. In the morning, I went to the small, nearby village. I still had a few Marks on me. I bought bread from a peasant woman, and at the same opportunity, asked how to get to the road to Grodno. That, she didn't know, but if I was looking for housework and farm work, she could help me with that. "My relative in the neighboring village would be happy to hire a Polish woman to work. She is on her own and she is also not in good health."

I went, happy inside that I'd found such bountiful treasure. The village wasn't all that close, it was even quite far away. I arrived safely at my destination, at the woman's relative. She asked me who I was, interrogating me as to who, what, where and when." "I'm a Polish woman from White Russia," I told her, "The Germans took me, along with other Polish women and girls to work in Germany. I managed to escape from the nearby train station. Why should I go to work for the people who hate us? My luggage and belongings and papers were left on the train with the Germans. I can't go home, because my city has already been occupied by the Russians."

The woman was very moved by my story and harsh fate.

She, herself, did not need help as she was going out of town. But she wouldn't leave me to alone. She would find employment for me with someone else. That was what a Polish patriot like me deserved! She wished that all the Polish girls who were sent to work, so to speak, would do the same, since they were placed in brothels.

"What do those Germans want from the poor Polish people? Was anyone stopping them from shooting all the

Jews? In that, the Germans had actually brought great benefit. It's a pleasure now, to stroll through the village, in the market square, there isn't a single Jew there. They're all our own people. Now there are only Christians in the Jewish houses, in their stores, in their beer cellars. Our kinsfolk. But may the Lithuanians drop dead. They took all the good homes and businesses of the wealthy Jews and kept them for themselves. Still, don't despair! Our *chłopcy*, our Polish youth, have already got organized. They won't let them do us any wrong..."

And so, she sat and poured her heart out to me. She was only sorry that I hadn't come to her the day before, or the following day. Then she could have introduced me to some John Doe. Today, she was busy. There was a meeting in the next village of activists from the whole vicinity. She wanted to be there, and also had to be there. She gave me the address of another farm. There, I could work without papers. They were all people of our own there. And since evening had already fallen, she would accompany me to her relative at the edge of the village, to arrange a place for me to stay for the night.

Her relative, an elderly peasant woman, was very concerned. Where could she let me sleep? Just that evening, she had her godson coming to stay with two of his friends. They were organizing the party for the activists in the neighboring village.

I told her that there was no need for her to be concerned. I had a place to stay in the village. My hosts would be very happy to see me. And I would also start working for them in the morning.

She was very happy to hear it, and advised me to be careful on the way, because there were so many spies around

- concealed Red partisans. Her acquaintance told her that some *Zhyd* woman had passed through the neighboring village. Oh, if only she'd fallen into the hands of the chłopcy! She wouldn't still be alive. The difficult times that were coming frightened her. She heard that the Bolsheviks were advancing with such great force, like a black cloud. Like a horde of Tatars. It was Satan himself who was helping them.

I kept my conversation with her short. But before I said goodbye to her, I told her not to worry so much. Because her hatred for the Bolsheviks wouldn't stop them from marching forward and her annoyance at them would only do harm to her health…

Morning found me already far away from the village of the Black Hundreds. Luckily for me, I'd got there when I did, and not the day before or after.

I returned to the steppe forests, but far away from the previous villages. looking at my little companion, the little basket in my hand, a passerby, a farmer, said to me: "Pani, you have no reason to go. The *chłopcy,* our partisans, have already left."

He assumed that I was bringing food to one of them, to the White partisans, as they called themselves.

"Is that for a son?"

I didn't answer him, and continued on my way.

14

It was Sunday morning. The villages were still asleep. Only the roosters were already crowing, making sounds of home, cock-a-doodle-doo, evoking longing…and envy. I came out in front of a tiny village of just a few houses. Who was there? Were they Polish, Lithuanian, or may God protect me, Germans?

The house closest to the forest was beautiful, with a number of windows placed at a symmetrical distance from each other, flower beds alongside the house, and in the middle of the yard - a rustic well.

I decided to rest in the woods in the meanwhile. What reason did I have to hurry? I didn't want to eat, and I couldn't sleep. I sat there and looked, watching the village, which had now woken up.

Young women walked off somewhere, probably to church. Out there in the distance, church bells rang. Something in their ring seemed to resonate in my heart, like a remnant of the pogroms against Jews in the distant and recent past, although I didn't believe that history repeated itself. It's simply that Jewish blood spills in every generation.

An elderly farmer came out of the nearby house and walked slowly toward the hut in the forest: a rural bathhouse.

I approached him and asked what the name of the area was. My question surprised him. "What do you mean, you don't know the name of the area, are you not from around here? If so, where are you from?"

I told him that I was on my way to Grodno, to acquaintances. I needed to get across the border and so I had set out on foot and taken a wrong turn. I didn't know where I was. He told me that he was Polish and that Grodno was still a long way away. The people in the vicinity were mixed: Lithuanians, Polish, and the old border between Poland and Lithuania was nearby. The Lithuanian guard was not far away. The long line of woods surrounding all the villages was the famous Rudniki Steppe. The road to Grodno crossed all the steppe forests. Lithuanian police swarmed and crawled through all the villages around there, whereas the Germans guarded all the railway lines. In the end, he invited me into his home, to his wife. I thanked him and said that perhaps I would pop in later. In the meantime, I would stay in the forest. And indeed, I sat there for a few more hours. I didn't know what to do. The steppe and its forests were drawing me, for some reason. After all, this was where the last partisans from the Vilnius ghetto had come. But how could I get there, when all the routes were so strictly guarded? Secondly, the steppe was as vast and wide as a desert. How could I find anyone there?

It seemed that I'd come quite a distance; many miles, in fact, and the partisans' forests were still very far away. I believed that I would run into the Jewish partisans from Vilnius in that part of the Rudniki Steppe. But how would I get there? My eyes were fooling me. It seemed that the further I went through the steppe forests, the further they were moving away from me. Like the golden ball in a children's story.

I passed by a stream. A man holding a fishing rod was sitting on a rock. I asked him if I was going in the right direction toward a certain point on the other side of the Grodno road.

The man looked like a peasant from one of the villages. He scrutinized me and said, "You're on the right track, but you mustn't go that way. The Polish partisans are here now. They suspect everyone. There are observation posts on every road and path. They're checking all documents and papers carefully."

I asked him why he was telling me that.

He hesitated for a moment before replying: "You're Jewish, a Zhyd. Your papers must certainly be fake."

Why should I withhold details from him? I thought, nodding.

The peasant advised me to backtrack and to stay as far away from such places as possible. He pointed in the direction where I may still be able to go. I thanked him and turned back. Going back meant going home, but where was my home? I was wandering around looking for it. Perhaps it was on the edge of the partisans' forest on the Rudniki Steppe.

I measured the miles and walked toward my previous places. I arrived there in the evening, tired and crushed. I still had one more route to follow into the forest. My legs and my body and my common sense all told me to stay where I was, and perhaps to even try to get some sleep. But the way that I was feeling gave me the energy to keep going. Forward, on, like the Wandering Jew.

I walked all the way through the forest and arrived at a big village. It stretched in every direction and bordered on the partisans' forests on one side. I knew that there was a locked synagogue in this village, with an open balcony.

By then, it was nighttime. I climbed over the railing. I put my head on my only friend - my basket, and fell into a dead sleep.

I woke up to the sound of gunshots. Bursts of gunshots. They were shooting on all sides. Dawn had broken and the sky had turned gray. I looked out carefully from my hiding place. The villagers were fleeing their homes, dragging bundles and sacks. The women carried their babies and children in their arms. They all ran into the partisan forest.

What reason did I have to sit there? I quickly left my shelter and ran off with everyone else. When I got to the woods, I felt more at home. The shooting stopped and the villagers returned to their homes. I stayed in the forest. Let them go back, I thought. That, too, was for the better. For me, being alone in the forest was the safest company I could have right then.

The exchange of fire was between the partisans and the Polish gangs. The latter had come through the same part of the forest that I'd passed through the day before. They moved close to the village, and there, the Red partisans showered them with bullets. The White Polish partisans were forced to retreat.

I thought about how I'd run frantically through the forest the day before. Those bandits had been right on my heels. It was their bad luck that I had a little luck.

I recalled the dream that I had when I was in the ghetto: I arrive at a mountain, on which a fire is raging. At the foot of the mountain, there is a sea of water. It's nighttime, and dark all around. It's a miracle that the fire on the mountain is lighting up slices of the dark water. That's where I have to go, and there is no path.

In my dream, I passed through fire and water, and continued on my way. Now, I was sitting in the forest under a tree, feeling as if I were in that bygone dream. And after it. In reality, however, I had not reached the end of my path.

The day moved on. I was hungry, I was living on bread and water, literally. Somehow, I could find water in the forest, but I could only buy bread in nearby villages.

I wasn't sure that was something I'd be able to do. But the hunger was not a guest who could be asked to leave. And so, between the thoughts about going or not going that were racing around inside me, I found myself by the nearest farmhouse. But in vain! The way was blocked to me: "So that the Russian refugees don't dare to enter the village!" They thought I was one of them. I tried my luck and went to the next house. The village was big, and the houses were far apart.

I was given the same reception and answer. "Refugees have nothing to look for here." And to frighten me off, they let their big dog off his chain. I had no choice. I returned to the forest without bread.

I could understand them, those farmers. On the one side, they had the Red partisans, and on the other, the White. They viewed the refugees as an unwritten plague. What did they care about a stranger who came knocking at their door? It was well known that a satisfied doesn't understand a hungry man.

And so, as I walked, forgotten by God and by people, a young farmer woman caught up with me. She was very happy to meet me. I was one of those refugees, one of the Russians. She'd heard that Russian women were experts at guessing cards. Someone had upset her lately. She was having bad moods, and she wanted the cards to save her; to tell her about the past and the future.

I tried to evade her. I told her that I didn't have my cards with me, and I could only guess correctly by using them. But none of my excuses were of any help. She had cards at home. She lived nearby and there was no one at home to disturb us. She led me through the garden, and the next thing I knew, we were on the terrace of her home. All around there were vegetables and flowers. The woman went to get the cards. I talked with her in the meanwhile, about this and that, trying to find out the cause of her pain. She revealed a little. The cards would continue to "find out" more. Unintentionally, she helped me with that. She suspected that her husband was cheating on her. She trusted the cards to reveal everything to her.

I spread the cards out and arranged them the way that the fortunetellers did, and then I told her what she wanted to hear: Her husband was not cheating on her, that was as clear as the sun. The only thing she had to do was to stop suspecting him and then she would be happy.

The woman was delighted with that conclusion. She brought me bread and milk. I told her not to go to too much trouble, the farmers in the area were complaining about their dire situation.

"Never mind," she dismissed it all with a wave of her hand, as if cleaning crumbs off a table, "the farmer is like a sheep who has been shaved all over but it all grows back again." She asked me to come back to see her with my cards. She hoped that my cards would bring her true salvation. She expected wonderful things from them. She led me out through the garden, and again, I found myself in the forest. The shepherds came with their animals at the crack of dawn. I was afraid of running into them and left immediately for a completely different part of the forest. I came out in front of a beautiful country home. Everything about it seemed quiet and peaceful. Pleasant. It had a fence around it and a lot of flowers. I moved closer. The dog, who was tied up, barked. He was calling his masters to come outside.

I asked for a little water to drink. Without saying a word, he brought me a glass of milk. Drink it, Pani. I'm sure you've already had plenty of water to drink."

His tone and manner were friendly. Humane. This was not something I'd found other farmers in the villages in the vicinity to be.

I asked if they needed any help on the farm and with housework. I also knew how to sew and knit, besides field-work, of course. He asked me to come inside to his mother. She ran the household. I went inside and was met by a kindly elderly woman. She was the image of a Godfearing woman, with a beaded band with a cross instead of a watch on her wrist - a Polish rosary. Again, I offered to help with whatever she may want, and if not, perhaps I could spend a few nights there.

She led me to a room and pointed at a Jewish boy of about three or four, who was playing quietly and serenely with a kitten. "You see," she said as she held her hands out, "the cross that I chose to bear I do so with love, but more than that would be difficult for me." The baby had been left with her so that she would save him. She had no idea if his parents were still alive. The boy called her Mama and was very attached to her.

Her son came in. He took the boy in his arms and went outside with him to the garden. The woman didn't ask me a thing. She could see that I was Jewish, and that was enough for her. She offered me something to eat. Then she accompanied me through the garden to the forest, wished me everything good and that God will protect me from all evil. On the way, she bowed down low to me. I returned to the forest, and as I walked, I wondered why she had done that. I couldn't understand it then.

Sometime later, I understood. After the liberation, when I was watching the Russian movie *The Undefeated, in which a Russian man bowed down before his Jewish acquaintance, after seeing him being led off to be shot, as if saying to himself, "It is not before you that I bow down, but to your great suffering." I remembered the farmwife, her innocent ways, and I realized: She was not bowing down before me, but before my suffering. She could see my bumpy path clearly. She may have seen Jesus on his tortured path to the cross in me. She may have seen me in her imagination being tortured to death, in the same way.*

I walked like that, deep in thought, through the forest, and that actually calmed me slightly. Suddenly, I ran into a party of partisans. There were five of them. Three of them were Jewish. One, from Vilnius, knew me by name. To me, it was as if he had fallen from the heavens. I briefly told him about my wanderings. He very much wanted to help me. Maybe they would welcome me at his camp. He would talk to the commander, and come back here the next day. I waited for him.

The second was a young man from a town in the Šiauliai district, and the third was from Częstochowa. He'd run away from Hitler to Lithuania, and again fallen into his murderous hands. He was one of 40 Jews who had recently fled to the partisans from the Kaunas area. Of the 40 who had fled, 37 survived. Three fell in battle.

The next day, my Vilnius partisan brought me the commander's decision: There was no room at the camp for me. The situation at the moment was very bad, but in the meantime, he'd arrange a place for me at a farmer's farm.

For me, that was a real lifesaver. I slept at that farmer for a few weeks, having to leave during the day.

Slowly, , good news filtered in from the fronts. The Red Army was already at the door. The moment of salvation was coming, of liberation from those bloodthirsty people, the Germans. Any moment, a light would be shining on us - on those who were sitting in the dark and in the shadow of death.

The Germans, before retreating, were still endeavoring and trying to eliminate the partisans. They didn't stop shelling the forests from the air. One day, the village I was staying in was bombed and shot at. The farmers boarded up their houses with planks and nails and dispersed to other villages. And again, I stood there with my little basket in hand on the edge of the forest. And again, I didn't know where to go. My dream of the partisans had come to an end. It was over and done with. In the villages where the "Whites" were lying in wait, they wouldn't hesitate to raise me on the cross, yes Jesus, no Jesus. As such, I decided to go back to the Lapinskis, like in the old days. Perhaps they would have some advice for me. They welcomed me with open arms. Good, it's good that I came. They were no longer afraid. Also, the Red Army was already on the threshold. Something had moved on the western front, too, according to the rumors. And the American and Allied armies were also no longer sitting back. In any case, they were already planning to welcome the heroic, conquering Red Army there. I could be in the barn, in the garden. After all, summer had arrived. And the Germans would be fleeing soon. The people in town were all absorbed by their own little worries and their joys, perhaps imagined, and also by the military and political news arriving from all directions. The Germans, in this area, had recruited the Lithuanian youth from the villages. Some of them had been sent to the front while others were sent to fight the partisans, mainly those on the Rudniki Steppe on the other side of the road - on the Lithuanian side. At that time, the White Poles started to sing more softly...

In Trakai, the Lithuanian General Plechavičius performed his last orders. In Vilnius on the Sunday of that week, the Lithuanians and the Polish clashed, both sides incited by the Germans. We heard about the dead and the wounded.

A few days after I returned to the Lapinskis, the Lithuanian fighting company passed through the village. Farmers transported their equipment, clothing, belongings, food and weapons on their carts. They settled in another village bordering the partisan forest. They moved into the bigger houses in the center of the village, and like "decent landlords" they sent the peasants with their carts safely home. They rested, ate their fill and then they all went to sleep. The next day, they would attack! Let the Germans learn from them how to eliminate gangs! Finally, neither the Germans or the Reds who came from afar knew their way around those swamps and forests the way they did. They, the Lithuanians, had been the lords of the place for generations. And they slept the sleep of the just.

But not my partisans. They didn't sleep. They didn't wait for the next day. They set fire to the houses where the Lithuanian heroes were sleeping, who got away by the skin of their teeth, naked and barefoot, and went to the neighboring houses. The cannons and machine guns and rifles thundered all night long. The next day, the German companies arrived to rescue the Lithuanians.

A few more days passed and a new Lithuanian company arrived in the village. They recruited all of the locals to dig trenches. They destroyed a number of houses that "stood in the way" and the Lithuanians dug down in the trenches.

The partisans in the forest greeted them with a shower of bullets. The Lithuanians responded with spicy curses.

Someone brought to the village a copy of the letter that the partisans had sent to the Lithuanian fighters. The letter said: "Lithuanian brothers, who are you going to lose your heads for, our eternal enemies, the Germans? Be smarter, be prudent, and come to us in the forest."

And wonders of wonders, the letter helped. A large part of the Lithuanians changed sides to the partisans in the forests.

Those who remained loyal to the Germans were taken by them. Then they shot the Lithuanian commander. They accused him of treason; of being a Russian agent. To make an example of him, he was shot in front of his Lithuanian soldiers.

15

Late June, 1944. The Red Army was advancing quickly on all lines of the broad front. Parts of two divisions from the White Russian front were approaching us. Everything was advancing. They bombed the iron-concrete and steel fortifications of the enemy. The Germans were the first to run, with their aides behind them. In their hasty retreat, they still had time to destroy and burn everything: roads, cities, farms. Again, the trains were not arriving at their stations. The last train was ready to set off with the last of the fleeing Germans, if they weren't too late.

On the quiet evening of July 9, 1944, the first Russian tanks were spotted close to the Rūdiškės Station. They appeared suddenly, as if by magic wand. The Russian cannons thundered throughout that summer night and the farmhouses wobbled with every barrage.

That night, I felt as if I had been reborn, as if a new life was springing forth from within me. The day that I had been waiting so expectantly for, was nearing. That's how I'd imagined the liberation. With blood and fire, lightning and thunder, life would return to what it was, like the stump of a flickering candle, close to its last breath.

The morning of July 10 the next day, was a bright, warm and sunny morning. I was free! There were no Germans, no Lithuanian police. No Akubazs. They had all been swept away by the wind. Everyone around seemed to be dancing and singing. I was free, free! Again, I was like everyone else in the world. I was human again! On that night, the Red Army marched forward and liberated all the territories in the area. Including the little village that I was staying in.

The noise of the tanks and other armored vehicles grew louder. The tank chains ironed the wide road and nearby dust roads. I ran over to greet my liberators, to wish them an easy and speedy victory over our bloody enemies, those animals in human form - the Germans and their aides.

On that day, the entire Rudniki Steppe and forests fell into the hands of the Russians. The partisan companies in the forests helped them to achieve this.

The Germans, in the throes of death on this part of the front, bombed the Rūdiškės train station. They destroyed and burned houses. They wanted to do now what they hadn't yet achieved. They also managed to slow down the Red Army's progress and even to stop it, but not for long. The Red Army was already experienced in such things and weren't impressed by the Germans' antics. They had time to breathe. Before we knew it, they had control of all roads, train intersections, forests, villages, cities and towns. They all fell into their hands like ripe fruit. All kinds of weapons flowed in after the army:

heavy and light cannons, Katyusha rockets, defense weapons, radar, kitchens, ambulances and more. They were on the way to East Prussia.

The "leftover" Germans emerged from their hiding places or from the village houses with their hands raised, looking forlorn, or making themselves look pitiful. They asked to be taken hostage. The Red Army personnel instructed them to report to places where people like them were registered, as was published in the orders. They didn't have time, the Red Army officers, to deal with such trifles; to answer unrelated questions. Other cities were waiting for them, such as Königsberg, Berlin...

July 13, 1944 was the day that Vilnius was liberated by the Red Army. On July 20, I said goodbye to my hosts, my good friends, the two humane Polish families, and left for my hometown - Vilnius.

When I left the places that I'd lived like a gypsy for that period of my life, I went to the fresh grave of the shot Jew from Rūdiškės. I didn't remember how to recite *Kadish* by heart, so I whispered a prayer of my own, from the bottom of my heart. Rescue had been so close, and he was murdered on its edge.

I traveled by car from the Rūdiškės station. A young Lithuanian partisan was on her way to Trakai and she gave me a lift to Landwarów. From there, I walked to Vilnius, about 12 miles. I imagined myself as a pilgrim in ancient times on a pilgrimage to Jerusalem. After all, Jewish Vilnius were famous throughout the Jewish world as the Jerusalem of Lithuania.

There was a lot of traffic on the main road to Kaunas, a parade of different types of vehicles full of soldiers. They were a mixture of a few parts of a brigade. It went on forever.

A lot of live German bombs had rolled on the grass by the roadside. They lay there so innocently by the red and black berries that had ripened. Closer to the city, at the junctions and crossroads, there were messages: Roads such and such have been cleared of bombs.

I felt relaxed on my walk. After all, I was going home. My faithful basket, my friend on my many wanders, was in my hand. It was hard for me to part from it, even now, after I'd been liberated. On my walk, I thought that if I ever parted from it, I would burn it solemnly and say a give a eulogy in its memory, as it so deserved.

16

Many miles were already behind me and I was getting closer to Vilnius. I crossed the woods. It was fenced off with barbed wire along its width. It was, after all the Ponary Forest - that long, deep forest in which all Jewish Vilnius had been murdered. So much Jewish blood had saturated its soil. I recalled what God had said to Cain, and I thought that I, too, was hearing the voice of my dear ones' blood shouting to me from the ground. This was where my first close relative was murdered - my younger brother. Here, my parents, my husband, my two married sisters with their large families had crumbled into the pit. Oh, a significant part of that forest was mine!

An entire gallery of people's faces drifted through my memory: relatives, friends, good neighbors and many of my acquaintances from near and far. Jews from Vilnius, from Poland, from Lithuania, from Ashmyany, from Švenčionys. Jews from all around. They all gave up their souls here in great suffering, tortured horrifically. Where were they all, the Jews of glorified Vilnius, the rabbis, the scholars and regular folk, the leaders and the talented, promising youths, whose parents hung so many hopes on…

I remembered the legend about Jerusalem on high, built entirely of gold, with the righteous sitting there and enjoying ultimate spiritual bliss, where the dead are resurrected…and that after all, Vilnius, too, was Jerusalem…the Jerusalem of Lithuania… one of the most magnificent Jewish communities in the world.

After that, I asked myself: *Why doesn't the grass grow red here? After it has absorbed so much blood in its guts. And why don't the trees here turn gray-white, from all that they saw and heard? So much suffering, blood and tears. So much human cruelty. Screams to God and to humankind - and their ears were deaf. No one heard.*

For a moment, I felt a desire for revenge against the cruel enemy rising up inside me. Then I suddenly saw before my eyes, the famous Vilnius singer, Lyuba Lewicka, singing before she died, "God, God, why did you abandon me…" but the tops of the tall pine trees swayed gently in the breeze as they whispered to each other, as if careful not to wake anyone in the forest.

My darling saints, I will visit you again to honor your memory. I will come to you with all the Jews of Vilnius who are still alive, to mourn your loss…

I then went to look for my children, my son and daughter, who may have survived and were still alive. I also wanted to congratulate my young, surviving friends who had joined the partisans, and all the other remaining refugees of the surviving remnants of the Jews of Vilnius.

My dear children! I beg your forgiveness for doubting that you survived. How could I have conjured up the words "may have." Surely you survived, and I hoped that we would even share days of joy and pleasure. We, the Jews, had always known how to live on after we buried our dead. And so we would continue until we were truly saved.

The din of tanks and cannons and mortars on the road was deafening, but I barely noticed it. I suddenly found myself remembering an old lullaby that I believed to be one of Leiyick's, the wonderful Jewish poet and playwright. Without listening to it, I would often sing it by my children's cribs, and sometimes, for whatever reason, I would have tears in my eyes.

The heir of the wanderer
Tore shreds from the heart;
Raisins and almonds
Became bitter...

Ay, liu, liu, bitter.
They are all poisonous.
My songs - like branches
That are drawn from the trunk.

On all lips
my blood spills like wine.
Ay liu, liu, for now
You will live, Amen.

I quickened my pace, as if someone really was waiting for me. But then I stopped beside a small roadside church. Instinctively, I looked for an unwritten sign: "Passerby, stop for a moment. Here, the blood of a Jewish girl was shed. Here, she was shot by a murderer, a wretched German." There was no such sign, but it seemed to wave before my eyes.

A Christian witness told me about it. He happened to be passing innocently by. It was in the fall of 1942, during the horrifying massacre of the Vilnius Jews. A young girl jumped from a truck loaded full of Jews. Her leg must have been badly injured, but she somehow managed to get to the church. There, a German ran over to her and shot her under the shadow of the cross. I tried to guess who that girl was. Perhaps she was one of my daughter's friends?

The image of the young student Leah Bloch appeared in my mind. She was a student at the aviation school in Vilnius. I was almost certain it was her. The date she died corresponded to that of Leah Bloch: October 27, 1941. The future pilot wanted to protect her young life. She wanted to live so that she could take revenge on the Amalek of today. For the murder of her family; for the extermination of the Jewish people. Sadly, she didn't survive, that beautiful, brave girl. She was, and then she was no more. She was taken when she was young.

I left that place that I found so very sad. After all, I was now on my way to life. I was going to look for my children; for my friends. I was going home, to my ruined, desolate home. I could already see Vilnius in the distance.

I was now standing on a hill overlooking Vilnius. The city lay in a valley. Who was I meant to find there? The wide asphalt on Legions Street shone from afar. One sunny day, a very large group of Jews had been transported to Ponary along that street. Beautiful, well-dressed children were deliberately chosen to walk in the lead, like an orchestra brightening up a parade.

A German walked a few steps ahead of them. He was an expert at it, maybe a professor of child psychology. With a stick he drew figure eights on the asphalt, like the figure eights in the air that glowed on the asphalt in the bright sun…

The children, tired and weary from the long walk, were fascinated by the white scribbles that the man was drawing, and walked quietly and calmly, as if on a school trip. Their parents walked behind them. They were all being led into a new ghetto, a sparkling clean one. It was a festive parade to satisfy the ears and eyes of the Christian spectators who crowded around to watch the spectacle. But the new ghetto, though rich in scenery and greenery and trees - his name is Ponary...

I arrived at the first suburb of the city at dusk. I was very tired and I sat on a bench to rest. Here, a woman I knew approached me. She was Polish. She was utterly amazed that I'd managed to survive. She could see that I was tired and she invited me to her home. I'd if I wanted to spend the night there. I accepted her invitation willingly. In any case, my life back in Vilnius would only begin the following morning.

That's where I heard that my parents' home, along with other Jewish homes, had been burned by the Germans before they fled. I'm not flustered by that at all. Those apartments, which had been so dear to me in those distant bygone days had long been empty and desolate to me. During the first stage, they removed all the living people from there.

Immediately following that, the Christian neighbors in the vicinity snatched them up and divided the inheritance between them, part by part, justly and honestly. Now I knew that I had no part or claim to even the ruins there.

My clothes and shoes had long been worn down from overuse, from wandering about for all those months. All I owned, 10 rubles, was enough to buy half a pound of black bread. That was what it cost in those days.

In the morning, I went straight into the city. The first Jew I met happened to be a partisan from Lithuania. He told me about the whereabouts of the Jewish partisans from Vilnius. I ran there like a person who is driven by demons and who truly believes it. My reunion with my young friends, the friends of my children, was full of joy and tears. My children had not yet arrived.

My daughter and another girl were going to join the partisans in the Rudniki Steppe. Their Aryan documents, with which they were supposed to get through the police checkpoints along the way, raised some suspicion. My daughter delayed leaving, looking for a way to take me with her. Just the two of us remained from the whole family and it was hard for her to leave me. "To leave me in the lurch." We didn't manage to arrange it in time, before the extermination began. My daughter was stopped on the road, and along with many other young women and girls, she was loaded into the carriages of a "direct" train to a concentration camp in Riga. And Riga had not yet been released.

My son, too, had not yet arrived. I was also told about those young partisans from Vilnius who would never return. They had fallen in battle with the enemy. They had died the death of heroes, those wonderful Jewish youths. Who wouldn't remember them to his very last day?

A few Jews had already arrived in the city, originally from Vilnius, and from other places. They all had their own survival stories, their own miracles. The financial situation of these remnants, in those first days after liberation, was bad; dire, even. They starved until they found work.

The Christian inhabitants of Vilnius did not welcome us Jews with bread and salt. Some would have gladly served us stones. For most of them, it was a great surprise to see Jewish partisans arriving, the sound of their even footsteps in their spiked military shoes echoing on the road, as if to say:

"We are here, we are here, we are here!"

Even in the eyes of the better Christian population, the Jews belonged in the past.

I visited old places, so familiar to me from my previous life, and all desolate and in ruins. There were piles of bricks and broken walls and rubble - and that's all. I also visited the ghetto area. I walked through the streets and alleys, which were full of broken walls and bricks from the buildings that had collapsed. Every broken brick wall, every door and window through which the enemy had barged in, even every stone on the street, seemed to speak and shout to me: "You, you who survived, you know better than anyone what happened here!"

17

At night, on the break of July 29, the Germans bombed Vilnius. It was a terrifying night. For hours, the city was shaken by the multitude of explosions. Many of the houses collapsed, and a lot of lives were lost. That night, two young Jewish women were also injured and died. They were partisans who had just returned from the forests: Bluma Markowicz and Hasia Tavardeen. They were the only survivors of large Vilnius families that were murdered earlier in Ponary by the Germans.

Meanwhile, life in Vilnius was difficult. We hoped that this would change. The Germans had also destroyed the power station and water pipes. We carried water a long way, from wells that had been forgotten for years. In the evenings, we usually sat in the dark. We couldn't always get candles, even the size of a Hanukkah candle. The railway lines had been destroyed and there were no means of transportation in the city.

Jews immediately looked for work, anyone who could. Factories and workshops had been opened under order of the Soviet-Lithuanian authorities. Naturally, the lack of electricity made it difficult to work, but they worked and produced what they could, using what was available. A lot of the city's residents registered for work. They were actively involved.

The bakeries were working, too. The authorities opened up a good number of cooperative grocery stores, and whoever had work no longer went hungry. There was no lack of jobs.

The front was still close, and we could still hear the cannons thundering. The city was partly in ruins, but life had begun to flow and pulsate through it.

The Jews of Vilnius organized a relief committee that dealt purely with Jewish affairs. It worked very efficiently for those days. All the Jews of Vilnius registered there, and the new ones from nearby also did. The story of everyone's rescues were recorded - everything that anyone had to tell. At the committee's request, all letters and postal items addressed to the Jews of Vilnius who were no longer with us were sent to them. Jews looking for other Jews met there. It also happened that Jews indeed found Jews instead of meeting them in the afterlife, as they had expected to and were even convinced it would happen...

I started working in a factory and I was making money. I already had food to eat. My problem at the time was a room to live in. And that was not a simple problem at all. The residents of the demolished neighborhoods were housed in the apartments that the Germans and their Lithuanian and Polish lackeys abandoned when they fled like mice. I received an answer: One person cannot be assigned an entire room, even though it wasn't my fault that I was all alone, without any family. That was what the situation and reality dictated.

The Vilnius partisans didn't wait for the edict to be announced. They took care of themselves and moved into apartments that had just been vacated. All the other Jews also managed, somchow, some in good apartments, others in apartments that weren't all that good. I was out of it, simply because I worked all day and didn't have time to look for a place to live. Meanwhile, I had temporary accommodation on Wanglowa Street.

One day, I came home from work to find the apartment locked. I tried to reach acquaintances on another street - and found the same thing. There wasn't a living soul there either.

What had happened? Those were tough times after the German bombardments, which left many victims. The living wanted to live. The last shelling was at night, and as such, when evening fell, the Christians hurried to the shelters that had been prepared in advance. Many Christians had moved to the villages. The Jews, most of whom were living in dangerous neighborhoods near the railway lines, had nothing of value in their apartments and rooms, and they were light and free spirits. In the evenings, they went wherever their feet carried them. I was extremely tired and didn't have the strength to move on. I had no choice and decided to go to a Christian acquaintance of mine on Fagolanka Street. They too, weren't home…I noticed people with bundles walking about, looking for safety…I recalled one of the stories by Shalom Asch, in which he described a Jewish grocer whose shop was empty. "What do you sell, Jew?" "I sell trust," he replied. The Jewish grocer meant, of course, trust in God. It is better to trust in God than to trust in generosity. But what did I know then about such matters, when I was dying to go to sleep?

A number of women were sitting by a wooden house nearby Zakret Forest. I asked if I could sit by them and maybe spend the night there sitting on the stairs.

I told them that all my housemates were in hiding. They agreed. And what of it? Did they care if I sat on the stairs? After that, other neighbors arrived. Men and women in high spirits. They joked around, told rude jokes from the underworld. I understood that I was dealing with thieves of the highest level. They were waiting for a bombardment so that they could go out to steal undisturbed. I pretended to be dozing, dropping my head from time to time. I felt as if I may really fall asleep soon. One woman remembered that she could actually give me a room in the house to spend one night. And indeed, she led me into a dark room and locked me in from the outside. I groped about in the dark. There was a bench and a table. And so, sitting on the bench, my head dropped to my forearms on the table. I slept like that all night. In the morning, someone unlocked the door. I slipped out to the quiet yard and onto the street. I didn't see any of the people from the night before. There was no one to thank for the restful night's sleep that I had had.

It was early in the morning. I walked the streets of Vilnius, which were quiet now. The night had passed peacefully and quietly, without bombardments.

I was angry with myself. Why was I being so idle? That was enough idleness! I needed a place of my own, a room to live in. I take a few days off from work. After all, I was no stranger to the city. I had known it for many years. And if I looked, I would find one. My work would pay off, all I had to do was have faith.

People gave me tips. Here, there, but there was nothing. It was all taken. People quicker than me had beaten me to it. The manager of one house, a White Russian, advised me: In his neighborhood, there was a small family of Jewish partisans, just two people all in all, with a relatively large apartment. They may agree to assign me a suitable corner. I went to the address that he gave me.

Indeed, the Jewish partisan and his wife had a free room, but he was thinking of giving it only to someone they knew. I asked him what I had to do to get to know them. And I thought to myself: Abba Kovner, the commander of the Jewish partisans from Vilnius, would surely put in a good word for me. But the partisan didn't wait until I introduced myself to him. He didn't care who or what I was. He didn't need new acquaintances. He stuck to what he considered important: Only someone who was a partisan!

I had no intention of arguing with them. And I certainly wasn't going to deny their li*neage. I said goodbye to them and thought,* What a pity, such a nice hat on such a stupid head.

I tried to go to the Jewish Community Council, which was temporarily located at 15 Mickiewicz Street. Jews went there all year round, regarding various matters: letters, registration, messages, information. Did our Jews lack for concerns? I asked everyone who came in for information. They gave me tips that made me no wiser. I also received offers. One was prepared to give me a secluded corner in his entrance room on condition that I clean the apartment every day. I retorted that I wasn't in a very good mood or feeling humorous enough to accept such an offer (by the way, they paid pennies in rent, if at all).

I received a more respectable offer from a middle-aged Jew. He had a nicely furnished room, on Zawalna Street. The entire courtyard had previously been Jewish. Now, Christians lived there. The Jewish occupants had all disappeared. The Jews had taken just one, small apartment, after its Lithuanian occupants fled with the Germans, and its small rooms were grabbed by Jews, both former partisans and just regular Jews. Although it was crowded, noisy and bustling, one doesn't get lost among Jews. And they even found a place for me to sleep.

My luck was still working for me. A Russian partisan was living in one of the rooms. One day, there was a major rainstorm and the room was completely flooded with water. The recent German bombardment had shaved the house of its windows and parts of its roof. The Russian moved to a Christian apartment, and the room became vacant.

Here, Codarov, my *nachal'nik*, or supervisor at work, came to my aid. She was a Russian woman and she really wanted to help me. She immediately issued a confiscation order for the room and I was right there, and the room immediately became mine. True, the windows had no panes, like open mouths, and holes in the roof above, like a Jewish sukkah, but I felt as if I'd found great treasure. After wandering around for so long, I had a corner of my own again. But the room was empty with nothing in it. I had no household belongings. I started from zero: I needed a table, chair, plate, pot, casserole dish. There were none to be bought yet. All the private stores were still closed. The municipal stores only sold groceries for the time being, in rations.

18

I decided to go to my ex-neighbors. Maybe they could return some of my household belongings that they had. I didn't pin much hope on them. And I certainly didn't expect big items, but I did think that they'd give me back just a few small household items. I found their addresses. Over time, they had moved apartments several times. They usually made better deals when Jews were cleared out of their apartments, and from time to time, they moved to a better apartment, from the selection available to them. They all did that, both the wealthy and the poor.

First, I went to my former housekeeper. I had given her a lot of things before I was evicted from my home.

In those days, the housekeepers of Jewish homes, all of them Christian, did very well for themselves. They were the first to grab the best apartments. I met Pani Dozorchinni by her home. Her old apartment had burned down. She was very happy that I'd survived, that I was alive.

I asked if she could perhaps return some of my belongings, and she told me that some had broken while she sold others to have money to live on. The things that had burned in her apartment, she would certainly return to me. She didn't invite me into her apartment. I realized that it wasn't because of hatred or rudeness. She must have had a lot of my belongings and didn't want me to see them. She was already accustomed to them. I didn't want to ruin her joy that I'd survived, that I was still alive. I said goodbye to her and left empty-handed.

Next, I went to my Number 1 neighbor. She was living in a beautiful Jewish apartment, with her entire household. She, too, had some of my belongings. I asked her to return some of them to me, but she was of a different opinion. Although she was happy to see me alive, she had even been certain that I'd survive, she angrily advised me that first of all I'd be better off collecting from those who had taken much more than she had. Anyway, I had done her a great injustice when I left for the ghetto, by giving household items that she very much needed to other neighbors, and she had benefited less than them all. It still angered her. I didn't say another word to her. She was certainly right. If I'd acted fairly, I would surely have compensated her with something even now.

My third visit was to a working woman. A widow with children. I went into her place only so that I wouldn't offend her. She was as important to me as all my other, good ex-neighbors. She, too, had things of mine. But now she didn't have any. She had sold them for bread. She had already moved to a third apartment that had once belonged to Jews, and she had many more beautiful things, but the Germans set the homes on fire and everything had burned. She again found herself poverty stricken.

I was so sorry for her bad luck. The apartment she was living in now really was empty, but the draughty room I was living in was much worse and emptier. I comforted her and told her that still, she did have some of my belongings, and that I now had nothing. Nothing. Her bedspread was mine, and so was the carpet by her bed, as were other small items.

Possibly, she said, but I couldn't take those from her. And anyway, why did I need such old things, when I could buy everything new? "The government is now yours. Stalin - he's yours. You're in the saddle!" That's what she said and what she thought. And she was sure in her heart that the government - was us. And that every other Jew was Stalin's cousin.

I reassured her that I wouldn't take anything from her. and that it didn't matter if she had a little or a lot. I would buy myself new things. I would write to Stalin.

I approached another of my neighbors, a Polish family. They were of a better class of people. I was friendly with them for a number of years. I myself had given them a considerable number of my belongings. Many of them were beautiful and very valuable, and I gave them to her as a gift. All the rest, they promised me, I could take back whenever I wanted. In the last few moments before we left our home to go to the ghetto, I had handed them a bag of groceries and asked them to keep them for me. I told them that I'd return soon to pick them up. I didn't know myself where the ghetto was located.

A few days after we were banished so cruelly, I left the ghetto, an act that was very dangerous and life-threatening. I could have been shot in the middle of the street. I went up to the family to get the groceries back. We expected to starve to death in the ghetto.

The gentle woman came out to me to the stairwell. What? A bag of groceries? She had no idea where it had disappeared to. How did I dare to come to them, didn't I know anything? I wasn't allowed to come to the Christians even though the Germans were all bandits, planning to kill all the Jews, and she didn't understand the point of dragging all the Jews to the ghetto first, to torture them. "After all, they could shoot everyone immediately!"

She would pray for an easy death for me and my family. "May God protect Poland," she crossed herself - and immediately disappeared, slamming the door behind her.

I had a change of heart and didn't go into her, nor to any of the other neighbors. Those who'd gained the most from me, from my property, were those who now hated me the most. They all would have wanted to see me shot.

I went back to my room. My head hung lower from the force of the new blow that I'd just received. Oh, how little humanity there was in people. The desire for Jewish property had swallowed it all up inside them.

I changed my mind the next day. I would go to her! I didn't miss seeing her that much, but I didn't care if she became irate at seeing me alive, despite her prayers for my sinful soul and for an easy death for me.

I went to see her. She knew that I was alive and well. She had been informed of it and she had already hidden and cleared everything away. She told me that she had none of my items. I could check for myself, all over the apartment.

She also told me that she, too, poor thing, had suffered greatly from that war. The Germans had shot her friend's son, a boy of 16, for no reason. On the last day before they retreated, a German stopped him on the street: "Are you Polish?" and he shot him on the spot.

I told her that I knew the boy and his family. And from her way of thinking and from her understanding, the situation wasn't so terrible. He must have had an easy death. After all, she must have prayed for his soul and suffered terribly for it, the poor thing. She continued talking modestly and miserably. I understood that I would see nothing back of what I'd left with her.

I tried to remind her of her honor. "I accept," I said to her, "that for every human society in general and for the Polish people in particular, if one receives a gift from someone, one gives a gift in return." So then, how could she compensate me now for the beautiful things that I once gave her, because I was left with nothing.". She was stunned, how could I even think of such a thing, at such difficult times for her? She couldn't afford to donate anything to me now. And I thought that I had to give her something else too, now, to keep her happy.

I left her home in contempt. Her husband was a high-ranking official at the municipality.

I tried to find my mother's caracal coat. She had left it with a Polish neighbor, who told me that she had paid her for the coat. Not much, just a loaf of rye bread, but then…she considered that payment. She didn't, God forbid, want to take the belongings from poor Jews. May God be her witness. But she did proclaim that she had paid…

Again, I left without a thing. I'd had enough of those delightful visits! After all, the heavens, too, had shown us no pity. And nor were there signs or inscriptions on the graves of our holy loved ones. Their ash had become dust. And I was shedding a tear for what? For a few lost belongings?

A few days later, I ran into one of my former neighbors. She asked me why I didn't come in to see her. She also had something of mine. But she had sold it a long time ago. She could give me "a few potatoes and vegetables from her garden". I thanked her. "I have no need. I buy what I need to live." She had no reason for an unclean conscience. She doesn't owe me anything and she didn't have to compensate me for anything. God would help us…

19

Time passed. And time takes care of what reason cannot…the city of Vilnius had taken on a different form. It was becoming more and more attractive. There was now both water and fire. The various streets that had been covered in rubble had all been cleared, and people could now pass through them, even by car. More cooperatives were being opened. More items were available, and household goods. All a person needed was money.

The first warehouse to open was for ceramic dishes. I immediately bought kitchen utensils there. How happy I was when I brought my first purchases to my room: a couple of brown clay plates, bowls, cups and even a flowerpot. It was nice work, but the clay was simple. The flower pot was put straight into service and already held flowers. After all, I was waiting for my children and they really loved flowers. Even in the dark ghetto, in our gloomy cell, we would see flowers from time to time. Or a green branch. A sign and reminder of life and liberty.

My Jewish neighbors, in the other rooms of the apartment, which were as empty and as meager as mine, followed my lead and purchased clay utensils for themselves. "Down with those old sardine boxes, or paper, from which we used to eat. Long live our clay utensils! Hurray!"

The only window in my room overlooked the old Jewish hospital in Szawelska Alley. Now it was being used as a field or temporary hospital and was full of sick people and injured people from the front.

The severely ill patients lay in the more remote rooms at the back. The windows of the front rooms were usually open, and I could see half-healthy soldiers from various countries. They had even a Jewish fighter from the front. The soldiers enjoyed themselves as much as they could. In the evenings, their own forces often held concerts there. I listened to marches, war songs and Russian love songs that very much matched my gloomy mood. They sang and played. The traveling cinema also came there and brought some joy and life to the ill and the wounded. The joy also flowed from there - out.

The Soviet authorities laid General Chernyakhovsky to rest in Vilnius. He was the liberator of Vilnius who had fallen on the front. He was buried with a large crowd and a festive procession, in a small park near Vilnius Street, and they placed a beautiful monument on his grave. The general's parents were Jews from Vilnius.

More Jews arrived in the city, survivors from the surrounding villages and from Lithuania, which had been liberated in the meanwhile. They refused to go back to their old, desolate homes in the cities and villages, which had mostly been destroyed. The few surviving people, orphaned and bereaved, felt more at home in Vilnius. Here, life was already slowly pulsating.

Of the many rabbis and rabbinical judges in Vilnius, only one, young rabbi survived. Rabbi Gustin. Of the many synagogues and Torah study halls in the city, only Choral Synagogue remained standing. That was due to the fact that the Germans had turned it into a medical warehouse.

The Jewish Community Council, which was established immediately after the city was liberated had changed its address and was now at 19 Deutsche Street. The Soviet-Lithuanian authorities recognized it as the council of the religious Jewish community, with Rabbi Gustin at its head.

After renovating a hall of the Choral Synagogue, the Community Council moved there, to 35 Zawalna Street.

On the first Day of Yom Kippur after the liberation, the remaining Jews gathered at the Great Synagogue of Vilnius to pray Kol Nidrei. That was the last time. The whole synagogue was in ruins, and about to collapse. It was demolished immediately after the holiday.

The synagogue's large courtyard was covered in the rubble of the walled houses around it.

The Community Council held a large funeral. They buried torn and trampled Torah scrolls and holy books collected from the small synagogues in the ghetto.

Time flowed by. The Red Army advanced in heavy battle with the enemy. The German resistance had not yet been completely broken. Still, all of Lithuania, Estonia and parts of Latvia had been liberated.

It is well known that many thousands of Vilnius Jews were taken to Estonia and Latvia to labor camps.

One autumn day, about a hundred Vilnius Jews arrived in Vilnius. They had managed to escape the camps in Estonia. They brought with them horrifying news of the shooting and burning by the Germans of the Jews of Vilnius in the Klooga labor camp in Estonia. They also told us about the situation of the Jews from other camps. Most of them were shot in Estonia. The rest were transferred to other death camps, in which the killing industry was more mechanized and effective.

One winter day, I saw a larger group of Jewish children, boys and girls aged 12 to 15. They were walking from the train station. I stopped in amazement. It had been a long time since Vilnius had seen Jewish children. I wanted to look at them. Where had they come from? I count the rows: There were about 80 children. The group instructors told me that they were schoolchildren from Vilnius and the vicinity. They had been sent to a summer colony in the spa town of Druskininkai in the spring of 1941. During the German invasion of the Russian borders on June 22, they managed to evacuate the children deep into the Soviet Union to an orphanage in Oryol, where they stayed for the duration of the war. Now they were on their way home. But their homes and parents and relatives were no longer alive. Their home was now the orphanage in Vilnius. Only one of the boys, the son of the engineer Truk, was found by his mother, who had survived the Holocaust.

The war was still going on. The battles were hard and bitter, but the Red Army kept advancing. They had already conquered East Prussia. The German front there had collapsed on its fortified lines. They were panicking and retreating deep back into their own land.

Thanks to the rapid occupation of East Prussia by the Soviet army, the few Jews who had survived the German death camps in that area were saved.

Several Jewish women from the liberated camps arrived in Vilnius. They were the first swallows to herald the coming of spring. Our spring was indeed near. The Germans received gifts of fire on all fronts. It was not long before the Russian and Polish troops liberated Poland, despite the heavy battles, and they stood at the gates of Germany and on German soil.

The Jews of Vilnius, those who had survived the camps, women and men, arrived back in their home city. They came mostly from Estonia and Latvia. They came home. They went looking for their friends, but, oh, they found no homes and no friends. Many of them left and moved to the big world. Perhaps there, they would find friends. Some of them tried to start new families in Vilnius, to found new homes.

A storm was raging among the Polish people living in Vilnius and the vicinity. A political storm that shook the walls of "Vilnius - *moja ojczyzna*" Vilnius, my homeland. My Polish ojczyzna, of course. Under the final, unchangeable agreement between the Soviet authorities and the new Polish government, Vilnius was to be the capital of Lithuania. All the Polish people, including Jewish Polish citizens, were entitled, "whoever so desired," to move to Poland. A Lithuanian-Polish committee was immediately set up to deal with those who wished to return to their homeland.

At first, the Polish people were in no hurry to leave Vilnius. They lacked nothing. They all spoke the same language. In the name of God. "He that sitteth on high shall not allow them to be wronged so; to hand over Vilnius, their ojczyzna, to the Lithuanians they so hated." But that was the verdict of the Russians, who began the October Revolution, immediately after it. And now, it was confirmed again. Finally, the Polish came to know that God had more important issues on His agenda to decide, and the Western Allies, especially the United States and Britain, would not divorce the Soviet Union because of its affiliation with one city, Vilnius.

Droves of Polish people left the city and moved to their beloved country Poland, where their true homes were and where they would also feel at home. The Lithuanian authorities made sincere efforts, some with overt joy and others disguised, to carry out the transportations as quickly as possible, for the convenience of their brethren, the Polish people. They made sure that they didn't, heaven forbid, lack food for the trip or any possible comfort. They also had freight cars at their disposal and they could take whatever belongings they wished to take with them. This included moveable belongings such as cattle, chickens, dogs and cats. Many Polish people sold some of their belongings. They had too much.

I bought a table with drawers from one of my Polish neighbors. She swore that the table was her sole property. It did not belong to the Jews, God forbid. The purely Polish table now adorned my room. I took the drawers out to clean and found a pair of tefillin stuck in one...

The Jewish citizens of Poland also registered for repatriation, much to the satisfaction of the Lithuanians. Their Vilnius was finally freeing itself of Jews, too, who had always been a thorn in their side. Only the Russians, colleagues of the

Jews from the factories and offices, wondered why the Jews preferred to go to Poland.

We talked between us. They asked me why we were leaving. "Have we caused you any injustice or harm, that you're going to the Poles, who hate you with their hearts and souls? Or do you perhaps not want to live in Lithuania? If so - Russia is so big!"

The Jews couldn't answer that question themselves either. But it was fact: Jews, mainly simple, working class people signed up for repatriation. Others, after a few days, regretted it: "We aren't going!" then a few weeks later, they changed their minds again. On the other hand, the Zionist youth were among the first to sign up. They set out even before the order was issued.

I was registered to go, but I didn't. I was still waiting for my children. The bloody war was coming to an end and I was still on my own. Why were my children dragging their feet?

My neighbors in the other rooms now changed. There were those who found a more comfortable apartment, and others left in search of their happiness in distant lands. They were replaced with Jews from Lithuania and White Russia.

My new neighbors in the rooms were Jews of three types:

There were those who survived the war in all sorts of ways, none of them easy, of course. There were Jews from Vilnius, who had survived the camps, and Jews from Lithuania, who had just returned from the Soviet Union. They all, every one of them, had miracles and wonders that God had done or not done to tell us about. Through their stories, I went with them from camp to camp - from *katzet* to *katzet*. I already knew it all. The camps, in all their forms, were terrible and awful. It was enough for generations to come… those who returned from the Soviet Union also had things to tell, about the harsh labor in Siberia, Astrakhan, Turkestan and Kazakhstan, and in faraway *kolkhozes* - collective farms. Most of the Lithuanian Jews were transported to places where there was a strict work regime. The only difference was that most of them talked about people who had survived.

Lithuania was now also liberated. Praise the Lord, the Creator of the new world! The Jews of Lithuania and their families went home. And everywhere, it was always the same: They once had homes, and their homes were no longer there. It was like a repetitive chorus. Even towns had disappeared. Like Jonava, for example, near Kaunas. The peasants from the surrounding villages demolished all of the houses and divided the land between them. They plowed and sowed and planted. And to be honest, if there were no Jews, what need was there for the ruins of their homes?

I met a large Jewish family who had returned from Russia. They, too, were from Lithuania. At first, they had difficulty understanding what had happened. How could one people destroy another people, in a land that wasn't theirs, and whom they had never known, for good or for bad. And they stood there and prayed to God, so that he may hear the blood-filled voices of His chosen people shouting at Him from the soil, and deliver them to their own land, the Land of Israel. And in light of the new situation that the Jews who had survived were now in, they were very worried and didn't know what to do or where to go to get by somehow. They didn't know whether to stay in Vilnius or to return to their own town or village, deeper in Lithuania. Or - one of the family members wished for himself, a little jokingly and very seriously - to stick the first peg of his new sukkah in his own country, the liberated and independent Land of Israel.

Another Jew from the same group, who had remained avowedly silent, received the right to speak. “My friend, what is this longwinded, futile debate for? One does not build new houses on land saturated with Jewish blood. Recent times have proven to us that we were saved thanks to the Kremlin edict to be exiled far from our homes because of our meager livelihoods, which were too big in their eyes, whereas the edict of God for us was to go to the Land of Israel where the blue and white flag fly over our homes...”

Two young Jews were living in another room. They had been disabled in the war against the German enemy for the homeland. They were both born in a town in nearby White Russia. They had recently left the hospital and they had friends visiting, who were also disabled. There, the discussions were about the fronts, difficult marches, attacks, fierce battles, acts of heroism and friends who had fallen. There was only one subject that they didn’t like to talk about: themselves. They, too, had had houses and parents and brothers and sisters and relatives and friends. And they, too, didn’t find a thing. And that was a fatal blow in itself.

Between one story and another of my neighbors in the other rooms of the apartment, I, too, recalled a few facts from those fateful days in 1941, when the Germans crossed the borders into the Soviet Union, Lithuania and Latvia, and the Jews there fled en masse to Russia’s borders. But those who fled to the Latvian-Russian border through the Daugavpils

District were not allowed to cross. For three, difficult days, those Jewish refugees stayed by the border, until an edict was received from the Kremlin to transfer them all to somewhere out in the back end of Asia, "To do important and efficient work." It was extremely harsh labor. But thanks to this, a few more Jews were saved. Many dozens of train carriages took Jews from Lithuania, Latvia and Poland to Turkestan, Kazakhstan and Uzbekistan. At the time, there was a popular saying in those countries: The Jews, without war, conquered Tashkent, the capital…

One fine day, my daughter arrived. She had escaped from the concentration camp in Latvia and found temporary refuge with a Latvian family in Riga. Her fate was almost like mine. My dear visitor fell on me as if from heaven. She, too, told her story and about her miracles.

Again, we were not alone. Again, we were a family.

But there was still no joy in our room.

20

The bloody war over the homeland had ended on all fronts. ON May 9, 1945, the Soviet Union and the Western Allies together achieved a complete victory over the Germans, Japanese and other enemies. It was a day of celebration all over the free world.

But I didn't celebrate. My heart weighed heavily on me. My only son Michael did not return. He had fallen in the forests of White Russia in a battle of a few against many, against the Germans and their aides. It was in the spring of 1943, and he was 24 years old at the time. He did not get to see the victory. The quiet hero with the fiery spirit, who encouraged and called on the Jewish youth to fight against the enemy. He, himself, fought until the last bullet, until he had lost all of his strength. His name was included in the list of outstanding fighters. He fell for the honor of the Jewish people, fighting for human freedom and liberty. I cried softly, but I may have emitted sounds of weeping, like the voice of Rachel when she wept over her sons, refusing to be comforted.

Many of the Jews of Vilnius who were Polish citizens eventually moved to Poland. They also took with them the Jewish children from the orphanages and other children whose parents, before being executed, managed to find refuge for them in a number of monasteries and Christian orphanages. They also managed to take back some of the children who had been handed over to Christian families. There was no information at all regarding some of these Jewish children, and the Christians who adopted them ignored the requests to give them back. All those children were taken to Poland, and from there, on. I believe that most of those children became good citizens of Israel. The Community Council kept accurate records of all the Jews who came and went, and of those who moved to Poland. There, too, there was a department maintaining historical records, where the two Rayak brothers from Glubokoye were very active. They asked anyone leaving, and those entering, to tell the stories about their miraculous survival, or to put it on paper themselves. The Rayak brothers also moved to Poland eventually, taking all the historical material they had collected about the annihilation of Jewish Vilnius, the surrounding Jewish communities, and more.

More Jews arrived in Vilnius, who had moved to the Soviet Union already in late 1939, when there were still no Germans on the border to stop them. They came from the distant ends of Asia, from beyond the Ural region and other places, including from the central Soviet Union. They returned from their service in the Red Army, the disabled from the hospitals. All the Jews of Vilnius were Polish citizens, and they flocked to Poland. But there were those who were tired of wandering about; who no longer had the strength to drag themselves off to places unknown, to the Land of Nod. It wasn't like they would build a city there, they said, only Cain could do that.

Most of the Jews of Lithuania and Latvia who survived the Holocaust returned to the Soviet Union, and because they had married Polish citizens, they also moved to Poland.

I traveled to West White Russia looking for traces of or information on my fallen son. The Akubazs, the fascist Polish gangs, and others, were still running rampant in the villages and forests in that area. They would lurk in wait for Russians and Jews and murder them ruthlessly. I returned to Vilnius with an aching and broken heart.

I met an elderly Jewish woman from Vilnius. She had just returned with three of her grandchildren, the children of her three sons, who had all fallen, like Red Army soldiers, at the fronts; one in defense of the road to Leningrad, the second near Kharkiv, and the third near the city of Raial with the Lithuanian battalion.

We didn't see the millions of Jews and other people who fell in the Holocaust and the war, and we would never see them again. They were sorely missed by their bereaved and orphaned families. We saw only those who survived - the victims, the war-disabled. The Jews among them, young people from Vilnius and from Lithuania, rushed home from the hospitals. Home. They believed that a loving, loyal hand would help them to dress their wounds, which had not all healed yet. Their disappointment was unbearable, a new wound in their hearts.

Happy was the disabled Jew who found a member of his

family. Most of the disabled Jews of Lithuania settled in Vilnius, where it felt more *haymish,* more like home. They were with their people. Most of them were soldiers from the Lithuanian Battalion.

There was now a disabled Jew living in the room next to mine. He had lost his whole arm. He was a Jewish boy from Kaunas, and was still very young. He remembered how, in 1941, his parents had fled their home in panic. It was an established and affluent home, and they were so happy to be allowed to cross the border into Russia along with other Lithuanian and Latvian Jews. They were sent to some remote hole, far away in Asia. But death found them there, too. His father was drafted by the Red Army and fell on the front. His mother was killed in a work accident. Next, it was his turn. He was drafted by the army. His little sister, Fraidaleh was left at one of the orphanages.

That was his story. Now his dear sister had come to him from faraway Turkestan. His beautiful little sister Fraidaleh. They talked. They joked. They enjoyed themselves. Youths will be youths. There was no one in the world happier than him. His disabled friends were jealous of him. They often said to him, "Good for you, you have Fraidaleh. We have no one."

Along with the Lithuanian Jews who returned, the father of two sons also returned. He was famous because of his sons. His older son organized the escape of 40 young Jews from Kaunas and got them safely to a partisan camp in the forests. It was a brave and rare operation, as all the roads were blocked and death lurked at every turn, as they were in one big minefield. But he, the hero himself, did not survive. He was tortured to death when he returned to save a few more Jews from the murderers. He was 25 at the time of his death.

His younger son, of 18, also died very tragically. Peasants caught him one night and imprisoned him in a rural prison, in order to hand him over to the Lithuanian police the next morning. It meant certain death. All night, the young man dug a tunnel under the wall and escaped. But his heart couldn't withstand the immense effort, and not far from his prison, he fell dead from a heart attack.

Those young people were not alone in the campaign of the Lithuanian Jews who fought for their lives and for liberty.

The Russian partisans from the forests of White Russia also returned, I visited them and asked them about my son. Maybe one of them had seen him, or met him. But White Russia was vast enough not to meet…

I could see my son in the disabled. My son. I visited a special home for the severely disabled and lonely. It was on Yaglona street. I saw a young Jewish blond boy, an amputee. He had two prostheses, and next to him two canes that he used to manage on his own. I looked at his blue eyes. They looked childlike. It also seemed to me that I could read his experiences in them. He was 15 when he left his home and family, his relatives and friends, in their distant Lithuanian town. Now he was sitting here, disabled - with what percentage? He noticed that I was looking at him and shook his fists angrily at me. I went over to him and asked, "Why are you angry at me?"

He apologized. He asked me for forgiveness. He thought that I was a Christian.

"And why are you angry at the Christians?"

"Why, why," he replied, and his blue eyes looked like he would soon start crying, "why, they killed my mother, my sister, my…and I'm all alone, like a rock…"

Indeed, I too often asked why.

My daughter got married to a former student at the Vilnius University. He, too, survived only by miracle. He fought at the front with a Red Army corps. He, too, had lost his entire family, an extensive Jewish family from Vilnius.

The transfer of the Polish people from Vilnius and the vicinity had been going on for a year and a half. More than 120 huge transports had already left, and the end was nowhere in sight. It was not over yet. Jews participated in almost every transfer…and we were in one that left one day in September, 1946. Our meager little bundles, compared to those of the Polish people, drew ridicule.

We looked at how the Polish were traveling so quietly and peacefully, confident and relaxed. And why not? They were going to their own country and homeland. And where were we going? Our country, the Land of Israel, was till closed to us, locked with seven locks and seventy-seven bolts.

We were going, supposedly, to Poland, right after the pogrom in Kielce. But we knew in our hearts: In Poland, we were merely passers-by, our eyes were set further away in the distance…

There were Jews who actually liked wandering around, traveling far to wherever caught their eye. "The whole world is at our feet. Why should we sit and wait?" But I was afraid. I was afraid of that "great big world" that was foreign to us, and hostile. We, the "remnants" who survived the terrible storm that had washed over us, the flood of blood that fell on us, we really needed and longed for our own, true home.

My daughter and son-in-law were actually feeling uplifted. They were overflowing with energy and confidence. The war and the Holocaust were behind them. Now, they were heading for a better tomorrow, one much more promising. That was what they thought and hoped, and were even sure of. Their hearts were sure that a fresh spirit was coming, and it would carry them to the Land of Israel, where they would build their home, "Literally, our home," they said.

And I? I went with the youngsters. Seeing them, my spirit was encouraged and grew younger.

Sarah and husband Shaul Shimonovitz before the war.

Sarah with her son Michael and her daughter Zuta in Vilna.

Members of Vilna's Ha-Shomer Ha-Tsa'ir movement.
Zuta in the center.

Sarah's younger brother, Zelig Torf, 1936.

The Jewish Street (In the small ghetto), Previous to WW II. From: "The Vanished World: Jewish Cities - Jewish People". Photo: R. Vishniak.
By courtesy of the Forward Association.

Glezer street, in Ghetto B (the small ghetto), postwar.
Photo by courtesy of Yad Vashem Photo Archive,
Jerusalem. 986/9.

FLIEGERHORSTKOMMANDANTUR WILNA-SÜD
ZERLEGEBETRIEB

Nr.

BESCHEINIGUNG

Der Jude Berkon Abram

wohnhaft in Wilna

ist in dem obg. Betriebe z. Zeit ständig beschäftigt und darf keinesfalls für andere Arbeiten verwendet werden.

Dieser Schein verliert seine Gültigkeit am 30./9. 41

sofern er nicht verlängert wird.

Wilna, den 22./8. 1941.

Techn. Inspektor

White Schein, the first work permit in the ghetto. Issued By a military work unit (The headquarters of airborne unit) on 22.8.41. Date of expiry: 30.9.41 Photo by courtesy of Yad Vashem Photo Archive, Jerusalem. 2074/70

The ruins of the building at 12 Straszuna Street where Sarah and her daughter lived for few months in the ghetto. This building also housed at that time members of the Headquarters of the FPO (United Partisans Organization) Jewish underground in the ghetto. The building was blown up by the Germans before the liquidation of the ghetto. Photo by courtesy of The Ghetto Fighters Museum, Israel / Photo Archive.

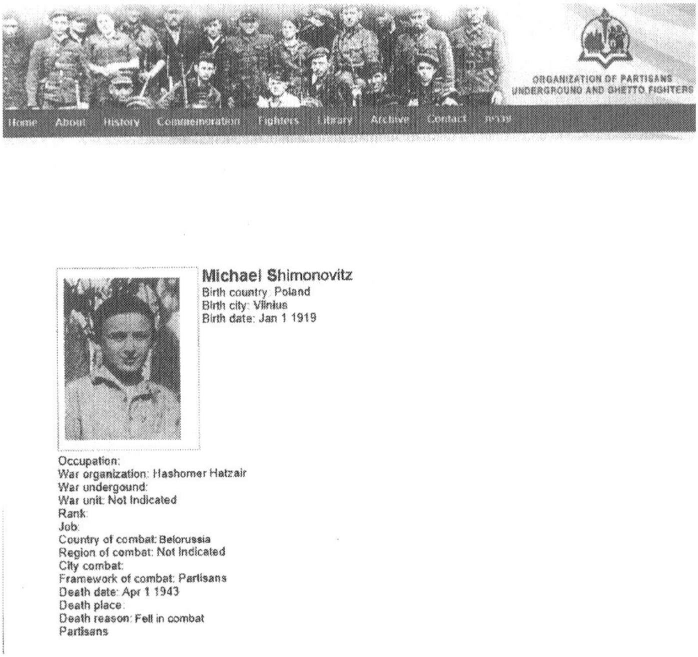

ORGANIZATION OF PARTISANS
UNDERGROUND AND GHETTO FIGHTERS
Home About History Commemoration Fighters Library Archive Contact
Michael Shimonovitz
Birth country: Poland
Birth city: Vilnius
Birth date: Jan 1 1919
Occupation:
War organization: Hashomer Hatzair
War undergound:
War unit: Not Indicated
Rank:
Job:
Country of combat: Belorussia
Region of combat: Not Indicated
City combat:
Framework of combat: Partisans
Death date: Apr 1 1943
Death place:
Death reason: Fell in combat
Partisans

Michael Shimonovitz, listed on the website of the Organization of Partisans Underground and Ghetto Fighters. Fell in combat in Belorussia, in 1943.

Sarah with Zuta and Zuta's husband, after the war, in Israel.

Certificate for planting thirty trees in the Jerusalem hills, in memory of Biseniece family members who saved Zuta's life during the Nazi occupation in Latvia, providing her with a hiding place in Riga.

די לעצטע יידן פון ווילנער געטא

(צוואנציק יאר פון חורבן ווילנע)

א קאפיטל זכרונות פון געטא־לעבן
פון שרה שמעונוביץ (תל אביב)

(המשך)

25־טן סעפטעמבער) שבת פרי.

מען טרייבט אונדז אויף דער גאס. וואס פירט צום באן. עס וואלגערן זיך פעקלעך, צעווארפענע זאכן, קינדער, איבערגעלאזטע, עלנטע, פארנעמען זיך מיט דעם. זיי וויינען דיכער הונגעריק און זוכן עפעס צו עסן.

מען ציילט אונדז צו 25 און מ׳פירט אונדז צום באן. איך קוק זיך אום, אפשר זע איך ערגעץ אנטלויפן? פלוצלונג באקום איך א קלאפ אין קאפ מיט א ביקס. מיר איז פינצטער געווארן אין די אויגן. פון דער פרישער וווּנד גיסט זיך בלוט. איך דריק צו די וווּנד מיט א טיכל און גיי ווייטער. און איידער וואס ווען, זיינען מיר שוין ביי די וואגאנעס. איצט אנטלויפן איז שוין אוממעגלעך. אונדז נעמען אריבער די אוקראינער. די ליטווישע פאליציי האט ווייטער אפגעטאן. מען האט אונדז ווידער געציילט דריי מאל צו 25. אויך קראנקע אריינגעטריבן אין דעם — צוזאמען 75 מאן אין אריינגעשפארט אין די קליינע בהמות־וואגאנען. די ענגשאפט איז געווען גרויס, ממש דערשטיקט צו ווערן.

אין דעם וואגאן, וווּ איך בין אריינגעפאלן זיינען געווען 2 קליינע פענצטערלעך גאנץ הויך. איך בין פון די ערשטע אינעם וואגאן און פארנעם גלייך אן ארט נעבן פענצטער. איך שטעל מיר אויף מיין פעקל, גרייך צום פענצטער און קוק פארזיכטיק ארויס. די אוקראינער — פון ולאסאוו ארמיי — דער פאררעטער גענעראל ולאסאוו באוואכן די שוין פול געפאקטע וואגאנעס. זיי זיינען גוט געשטימט. פאר זיי איז עס א פרייליכער יאריד. זיי דערציילן אונדז, אז מען פירט אונדז קיין ווארשע, אויף לייכטע ארבעט. מיר וועלן זיין אין וועג 4 טעג און מען וועט אונדז געבן ברויט מיט וואסער אויפן וועג. זייער פיינע לייט... מער נישט. מיר האבן זיך געווארפן ביים מיט די ראלן. זיי דערציילן ווייטער: אז האבן זיי נישט לאנג געפירט א גאנצן עשאלאן יידן פון עסטלאנד, אויף דער זעלבער ארבעט, אין ווארשע.

יא, מיר קענען זיי גלויבן. אין עסטלאנד זיינען אפשר נישטא אזעלכע טויט־לאגערן ווי אין דער געבענטשטער מדינה פוילן.

איך קוק נאך אלץ ארויס פונעם פענצטערל. די וואגאנעס זיינען אויסגעדרייט אין א האלבקרייז. מען ברענגט צו נייע וואגאנעס. מען פירט נאך אלץ אנדערע געטא־מענטשן: יונגע, אלטע, קינדער. זיי קוקן מיט שרעק, וווּהין פירט מען זיי? ווי וועט מען זיי אומברענגען? נאענט, אדער ווייטער א ביסל? זיי ווייסן, אז דאס איז זייער לעצטע נסיעה.

איך צייל 64 וואגאנעס, פולע, אנגעפאקטע ביז איבער די ברעגן, האבן אבער דאך נישט געקאנט אריינגעמען די אלע יידן פון געטא. א טייל האט מען דערווייל פארשפארט אין א געמויערטער געביידע נעבן באן. מען וועט זיי פירן מארגן. איך זע פון דער ווייטן ווי מען פירט זיי. דאס זעלבע בילד, וואס נעכטן: יונגע, אלטע, קינדער, מענטשן מיט פעקלעך, אן פעקלעך. אזוי גייען זיי צו דער שחיטה.

געבליבן אין שטאט זיינען נאר צוויי ארבעטס־לאגערן מיט יידן, די לאגערן „קיילים" און ה.ק.פ., וועלכע האבן געהאט זייערע אייגענע בלוטיקע געשיכטע.

דערווייל האט מען שוין דא דערלאנגט דעם לאקאמאטיוו. פונקט קומט אויס, אז מיין וואגאן איז דער נאענטסטער צום לאקאמאטיוו. אין צווייטן — אן אפענער וואגאן פאר דער וואך, פאר די אוקראינער. זייער נישט קיין אנגענעמע שכנים פאר מיר.

מיין געדאנק צו אנטלויפן לאזט מיך נישט אפ. דורך דער טיר איז אוממעגלעך. בלייבט דאס קליינע פענצטערל. דאר בין איך, הויט און ביינער. אויב ס׳וועט מיך נישט דערשיסן פריער, וועל איך פרוּוון מיין מזל אין דער פינצטערניש פון דער נאכט.

אלי ירחם...

(המשך קומט)

Excerpt from the original Yiddish material of the book, published in the newspaper Haint in South America in 1963.

My Mother

My mother and I were the only survivors of our family in Vilna. In the middle of the night, my mother jumped from a train headed for the extermination camp and I managed to escape from a work camp near Riga. The escape was just as dangerous. My mother became brave and was sure of her decision: "Do not die – live" and jumped.

My mother returned to liberated Vilna in 1944 where she began immediately to search for me. She followed every hint, every shred of information and rumor from people who had returned from the camps until she reached Riga, to people who had hidden me for a while. They had no idea where I had gone and she had no choice but to leave them with a photograph of herself.

In my escape I reached Northern Latvia and was liberated from the Nazi threat only at the end of the war, on September 5, 1945, in a small town in Kurland. When I returned to Riga, after a few months to the people who had provided me with a hiding place, I discovered everything; I found the picture my mother had left for me... and again, I had a mother.

We arrived in Israel in 1949 and the moment we had pretty much settled in, my mother began writing her memories. To this day, I can still remember her sitting day and night, writing and erasing and typing again, steadfastly and devotedly.

What she wrote did not get published for decades. One copy went to Yad Vashem and portions were published in a Yiddish newspaper abroad.

After her death, I decided to publish my mother's memories. In honor of her extraordinary and regal personality. Her tragedy and the tragedy of the Jewish people from a personal standpoint – as they occurred. She wrote them down for her and for her family and for the next generations. It is also in memory of the Jewish Vilna that was destroyed and will never be the same again.

Zuta Averbach-Shimonovitz

Written by the author's daughter in the Hebrew edition which she published in 1989.

Made in the USA
Las Vegas, NV
23 March 2023

69600766R00087